LOCOMOTION PAPERS   NUMBER

THE
LOUTH TO BARDNEY BRANCH

by
A. J. Ludlam and W. B. Herbert

THE OAKWOOD PRESS

© 1987 Oakwood Press (Second Edition)

ISBN 0 85361 348 6

Printed and bound by Bocardo Press Limited, Oxford

First Edition published 1984
Second Enlarged Edition 1987

All rights reserved. No part of this book may be reproduced or transmitted in any form or by any means, electronic or mechanical, including photocopying, recording or by any information storage and retrieval system, without permission from the Publisher in writing.

Acknowledgements

The Louth and Lincoln Railway, G.Y. Hemingway, Railway and Canal Historical Society, November, 1977.
The Great Northern Railway, John Wrottesley, Batsford 1981.
Locomotives at the Grouping, Casserley and Johnson, Ian Allan 1966.
Locomotives of the LNER, published by the RCTS.
The Great Northern Railway Society.
The Lincolnshire Archives, The Castle, Lincoln.
Grimsby Evening Telegraph.
Louth Reference Library.
Bill Abbott.
Tom Ayre.
Peter Chapman.
James Dales.
Marshal Dale.
Chris Duffell.
Pam Gooderham.
J.T. Howard-Turner.
Jim Jackson.
Paul King.
Eric Neve.
Michael Rogers.
R.G.C. Stephenson.

Special thanks to Mike Black for his remarkable photos of the line. This book, like its predecessor, is dedicated to Bill Abbott and the memory of the late Tom Ayre, as well as all those whose personal memories brought the dry facts to life.

Published by
The OAKWOOD PRESS
P.O.Box 122, Headington, Oxford.

The Louth to Bardney Branch

Contents

	Foreword	4
Chapter 1	The Louth and Lincoln Railway Company	7
Chapter 2	Operation of the Line	15
Chapter 3	The Line at Work	28
Chapter 4	The 1946 Explosion	42
Chapter 5	The Final Days	43
Chapter 6	Closure and Afterwards	46
Chapter 7	The Line Today	48
Appendix One	Louth to Bardney Engineering Works	50
Appendix Two	Signalling Plans of Intermediate Stations	52

Introduction

The County of Lincolnshire provided a haven for aging locomotives and rolling stock in their retirement from the rigours of, for example, the London Suburban services. It offered the prospect of years of not too demanding labour in the pleasant Lincolnshire countryside. Once away from the main lines a dive into rural Lincolnshire was like a step back in time, a real living museum. Carried by elderly coaches with dusty faded seats, usually pulled by a hump-backed, wheezing 'C12' tank engine, and passing through stations and past signals largely unaltered since the line was opened, it always seemed that the railway in rural areas was dominated by the life of the country rather than vice-versa. The intruder succumbs to the life of the local community and soon becomes part of the natural way of things.

The work of the ancients on the branch lines was sometimes rudely interrupted for short periods whilst the railway company experimented with different types of motive power. The ex-Great Central Railway class 'A5', 4–6–2 tank engines are reputed to have had such trials over the Bardney line. A Sentinel railcar worked on the branch in the 1930s. The distinctive lines of a Great Western Railway diesel railcar was seen on many Lincolnshire lines in 1952, used to help ascertain the kind of diesel power required in Lincolnshire. These were, however, brief interludes in what remained an unchanged scene for several decades.

Since the publication of the first edition of *The Louth to Bardney Branch*, more photographs and information about the branch have become available and are included here. That the first edition sold out very quickly after its appearance in 1984 is, we believe, justification for our belief that the railways of rural Lincolnshire had been sadly neglected by historians and that it was time something was done about it before it was too late. Since the appearance of the first edition there has been a veritable outpouring of books dealing with Lincolnshire lines. It is a pleasure, therefore, to offer the reader a revised edition of what proved to be the first of several books concerned with the branch railways of Lincolnshire.

A.J. Ludlam 1986

Foreword

It is appropriate that the foreword to this edition should be by Marshal Dale, a farmer, user of the line and an outspoken critic of its closure.

Being the son of a farmer with a well established large farm in the Binbrook area of Lincolnshire, I was somewhat surprised when my Father announced that he had taken a farm near Louth with a railway running right by it. This was in 1940, at the outset of World War II, the Ministry of Agriculture was telling farmers to grow certain crops which were in short supply at the time. Father decided that a move close to the railway would make his sugar beet crop more profitable as it cost only 4s. 6d. a ton delivered to Bardney by rail compared with 6s. by road.

Apart from the sugar beet crop the line was little used by us at this time. I do, however, remember having a Lincoln Red bull I had purchased at Lincoln Fair sent to Hallington by rail. Later, in 1947 when we decided to plant strawberry and gooseberry crops, most of the produce was put on the train at Hallington to be taken to Boston and Wisbech. Here the main sales took place, the crop being bought for canning or jam making.

I got to know the last station master at Hallington, Bob Cox, very well. Bob kept his garden alongside the line immaculate, having plenty of time to do so with only two or three trains a day each way. Bob recently retired from Market Rasen station. A predecessor of Bob's at Hallington used to get himself into hot water with repeated regularity. The problem was his inability to arise in the mornings in time to unlock the crossing gates. Drivers liked to keep a good turn of speed going to cope with the steep incline to Withcall. Being stopped at the Hallington gates resulted in the morning air being assailed by language which was quite unrepeatable.

Another good friend was the Reverend Wyer-Honey, of Raithby, who used the line to transport two or three of his hunting horses to meets in the Hainton, Wragby and Willingham areas, as well as the Burton Hunt nearer Lincoln. Of course, he would try to encourage the huntsmen to arrange the final run of the day in the direction of the Louth area, thus saving himself a long hack back. The good clergyman's *Daily Telegraph* and *Times* newspapers would be collected from Hallington Station at 8.20 am.

The threat of closure notices made all of us concerned as to the effect such an act would have on us personally. As well as transport for my sugar beet and fruit crops, the passing trains, in close liaison with my tummy, usually reminded me when mealtimes were due.

Finally, when the last passenger train was announced, we decided to organise a trip. I believe about twenty of us did the journey to Lincoln in the morning and returned on the appropriate train in the afternoon. A good time was had by all, including the pleasure of drinking champagne on the move.

Marshal Dale, 1986

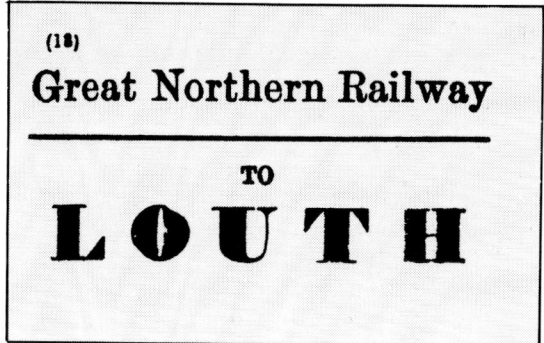

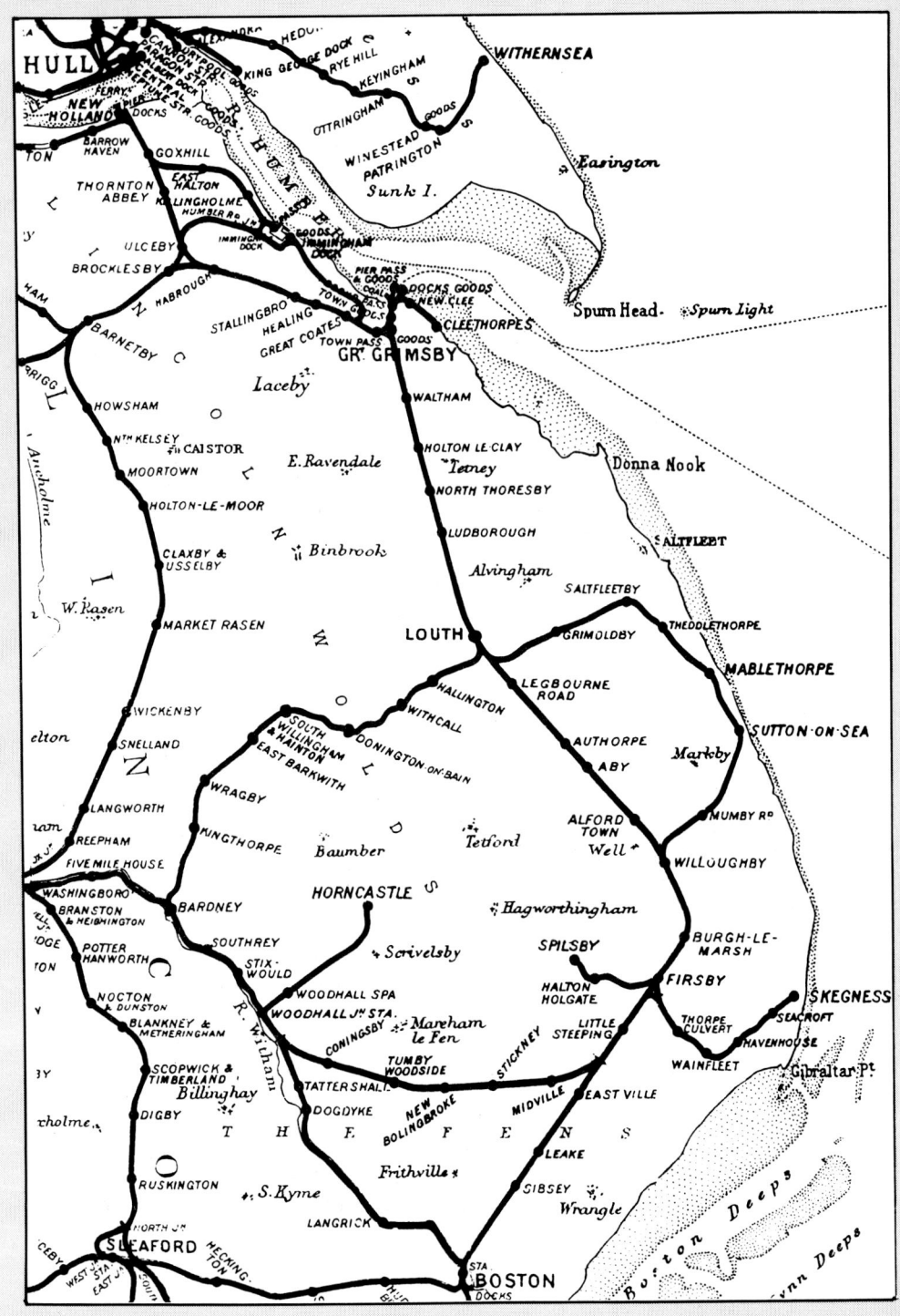

Chapter One

The Louth and Lincoln Railway Company

At a public meeting at the King's Head Hotel in Louth on 3rd November, 1865 it was unanimously agreed to investigate the possibilities of building a railway from Louth, via Wragby to Lincoln. Mr Heneage, the largest landowner in the district, agreed to act as Chairman of the provisional committee.

By 16th November a route had been approved. Leaving the East Lincolnshire Branch of the Great Northern Railway by a junction facing Louth, near to Monks Dyke Crossing, it would run south of Hallington, north of Donington-on-Bain, south of South Willingham and East and West Barkwith, north of Wragby to the south of Spring Wood and finally in a generally south west direction to cross the GN Loop line and terminate in a junction with the down line a short distance to the east of Five Mile House station and facing towards Lincoln. It was anticipated that work at either end of the line would be relatively light but, to avoid tunnelling, the eight miles of the middle section would involve mountainous gradients of 1 in 50 over a 1½ miles section and cuttings of up to 70 ft in depth.

The Louth and Lincoln Railway Company was incorporated on 6th August, 1866 with Capital of £250,000 and Mortgage Debentures of £83,000. However, by April 1867 the Directors were reporting that difficulties and problems over the purchase of land had made it impossible to join the Great Northern loop at Five Mile House. Consultations with the GN to find a solution were requested. After a long delay the Directors reported a disappointing local response to the raising of subscriptions. They unanimously agreed to ask the Board of Trade for permission to abandon the whole project. The application to wind up the company was made in 1870, but was refused.

The next important meeting of the somewhat reluctant company was in April 1871 when it was decided to go ahead with the project.

An agreement with a Manchester civil engineer, Mr Frederick Appleby, was signed. The agreement gave the whole capital of the company and its borrowing powers to that gentleman. In return Mr Appleby was to be solely responsible for the financing, purchasing, paying for and conveying the land. The Engineers Mr Myers and Mr Tolme were to construct the single line using 72 lb. rail, and in accordance with the 1866 agreement with the GN in which the GN had agreed to operate the line, providing it was certified satisfactory by the Board of Trade Inspector on completion. The line was to be completed in three years.

The Louth and Lincoln Railway Company.

Certificate of the Board of Trade for Authority to raise Additional Capital.

WHEREAS the Louth and Lincoln Railway Company have complied with the requirements of "The Railway Companies Powers Act, 1864:"

Now, therefore, the Board of Trade do, by this their Certificate, in pursuance of the said Act, as amended by "The Railways (Powers and Construction) Acts, 1864, Amendment Act, 1870," and by virtue and in exercise of the powers thereby in them vested, and of every other power enabling them in this behalf, certify as follows:—

Power to raise Additional Capital.

1. The Louth and Lincoln Railway Company (hereinafter called "the Company") are hereby authorised to raise, for the purposes of their undertaking, in addition to the capital already authorised to be raised by them, any further sums not exceeding in the whole twenty-seven thousand pounds, by the issue of new shares or new stock, either ordinary or preference, or partly ordinary and partly preference, at the option of the Company.

Incorporation of Companies Act, 1867, as to Shares.

2. In respect of any shares or stock to be issued under this Certificate, Section 21 of the Companies Clauses Act, 1863, shall, for the purposes of this Certificate, be read and have effect as provided with respect to a special Act by Section 27 of the Railway Companies Act, 1867.

Votes and Liabilities of new Shareholders.

3. Save as herein, or in or under the authority of the Acts incorporated herewith otherwise provided, the holders of shares or stock in the additional capital hereby authorised to be raised, shall be entitled to the like rights and privileges, and be subject to the like liabilities, as the holders of shares or stock in the existing ordinary capital of the Company.

Power to Borrow.

4. The Company may raise by borrowing on mortgage for the purposes of their undertaking any sums, in addition to the money they are already authorised to borrow, not exceeding in the whole nine thousand pounds.

Priority of Preference Dividend.

5. The preferential dividend or interest, on any new shares or new stock created under this Certificate, shall be paid in priority over the dividend or interest on the ordinary share capital of the Company.

Arrears may be Enforced by Appointment of a Receiver.

6. The mortgagees under this Certificate may enforce payment of arrears of principal and interest due on their mortgages by the appointment of a receiver; and in order to authorise the appointment of a receiver in the event of the principal money or interest due on such mortgages not being duly paid, the amount owing to the mortgagees by whom the application for a receiver shall be made shall be not less than nine hundred pounds in the whole.

Priority of Existing Mortgages.

7. Every mortgage granted by the Company in pursuance of the powers of any Act of Parliament, and in force when this Certificate comes into operation, shall have priority over all mortgages granted under this Certificate.

Power to issue Debenture Stock.

8. In respect of any part of the money hereby authorised to be raised by mortgage, the Company may create and issue debenture stock.

Incorporation of Companies Act, 1867, as to Loan Capital.

9. The sections numbered 23 to 26 inclusive, of the Railway Companies Act, 1867, with reference to loan capital, shall be incorporated with this Certificate, and shall apply to loan capital raised under this Certificate in like manner as if this Certificate were a special Act.

Costs to be paid by Company.

10. All the costs, charges, and expenses of and incidental to the preparing and procuring this Certificate shall be paid by the Company.

Short Title.

11. This Certificate may be cited as "The Louth and Lincoln Railway (Additional Capital) Certificate, 1875."

Dated the 19th day of April, 1875.

T. H. Farrer,
Secretary to the Board of Trade.

The Board of Trade, Whitehall.

Optimism was the keyword of the Prospectus. The Louth and Lincoln Company were confident in the assurance that the GN would operate the railway, but the GN exacted a price for their involvement, namely 50% of the gross receipts. 20,000 £10 shares were to be issued up to 1st May, 1872. The 24 mile line would serve, as well as local passenger traffic, visitors from the Midlands journeying to Cleethorpes. By using the Louth and Lincoln line a saving of three hours would be made over alternative routes to Boston or Lincoln, Market Rasen and Grimsby. No one seemed to question this doubtful claim. That traffic would be diverted from much better graded double lines, already working, in order to save a few hours was a hope rather than a fact, and was just as strong an argument for possible failure of the Louth and Lincoln should agreements to divert traffic on the new line not be realised with the GN.

The Prospectus made elaborate claims for freight traffic from the Nottinghamshire, Derbyshire and Erewash Valley coalfields. A mining engineer, Mr Roseby, estimated that there were 35,000,000 tons of good quality ironstone per square mile near Apley and 9,000,000 tons per square mile near Donington. There was talk of blast furnaces which would, if built, compete with any in the Country in the manufacture of pig iron. The potential was limitless, euphoria reigned supreme, the Louth and Lincoln was sitting upon a gold mine or so it seemed. The estimated annual revenue of the Louth and Lincoln Railway Company was given as follows:

300,000 tons of Coal at 5s. 8d. per ton per mile over the whole line	= £18,750
250,000 tons of Ironstone at 5s. 8d. per ton over 14 miles	= £9,114
Passenger and ordinary Goods Traffic	= £30,000

This made a grand total of £57,864, half of which (less 5% on the £83,000 Mortgage Debenture Capital) would leave £24,782 to give around 10% on the whole Ordinary Share Capital.

A revised route was proposed shortening the line to a final length of 20 miles and including two tunnels, one 803 yards long near Withcall and the other 255 yards long near South Willingham. Beyond South Willingham the line would turn more towards the south than originally proposed and join the GN loop north of Bardney station. Although the gradients were not as steep as the original plan they were still pretty considerable, with stretches between 1 in 66 and 1 in 76. Instead of all roads being crossed on the level, many now passed over or under the line. At Bardney the junction was reversed so that all trains ran into a bay platform, access to the loop being by means of cross-overs only. This meant that trains from Louth would have to reverse here.

ANNO VICESIMO NONO & TRICESIMO

VICTORIÆ REGINÆ.

****

Cap. cccxliv.

An Act for making a Railway in *Lincolnshire* from *Louth* to the *Five-mile House* Station of the *Great Northern* Railway (Loop Line), to be called "the *Louth and Lincoln* Railway."

[6th *August* 1866.]

WHEREAS the making of a Railway in *Lincolnshire* from *Louth* to *Lincoln* would be of great local and public Advantage: And whereas the several Persons in that Behalf in this Act named, with others, are willing at their own Expense to carry the Undertaking into execution on being incorporated into a Company (in this Act called "the Company") for that Purpose: And whereas Plans and Sections of the Railway by this Act authorized showing the Line and Levels thereof, and also a Book of Reference to the Plans containing the Names of the Owners or reputed Owners, Lessees or reputed Lessees, and Occupiers of the Lands to be taken for the Purposes thereof, have been deposited with the Clerks of the Peace for the *Kesteven* and *Lindsey* Divisions of the County of *Lincoln*, and such Plans, Sections, and Book of Reference are in this Act referred to as the deposited Plans, Sections, and Book of Reference: And whereas it is expedient that the Agreement contained in the Schedule hereto should be confirmed: And whereas the Objects of this Act cannot be effected without the Authority of

[*Local.*]   Parliament:

Although Royal Assent was not finally given for the change of route until the 19th July, 1872, Mr Appleby began work at the Louth end of the line in January of that year, confidently expecting, given favourable conditions, to complete the line in the ensuing year. Although the weather was not good, work was being pushed ahead steadily.

By the time approval for the change of route arrived in July, work on the deviated sections of the line was already well advanced. A 10 ft heading had been driven 90 odd yards at the east end and about the same at the west end of Withcall tunnel. The tunnel was being driven through sandstone and chalk considered favourable for tunnelling. Shafts and headings had also began on the shorter High Street tunnel near South Willingham.

At the beginning of 1873 work had slowed down because of excessive rain saturating the ground and making carting impossible. By August of the same year a delay of eight months was anticipated. However, the 10 miles or so between Bardney and South Willingham were complete and it was hoped would open by October. Work on the stations was progressing well and Withcall tunnel was within 30 yards of penetration.

It seemed Mr Appleby was having problems, and relations between him and the railway company were not good. Mr Appleby was accused of deliberately slowing down the work and the Directors resolved that unless some agreement could be worked out they would terminate the arrangements with him. The Louth and Lincoln agreed to take over the Works, the sub-contracts and Mr Appleby's obligations in respect of land transactions. Mr Appleby was to oversee the completion of the line.

By February 1874 the Engineer estimated that the line would be completed in three months. By May, however, he estimated that another £71,000 would have to be spent and so powers to increase the capital were sought. Meanwhile the GN had agreed to work the portion of the line from Bardney to South Willingham, but not under the 1866 Agreement which related to the whole line being completed.

In August the Louth and Lincoln reported the tunnels perforated and that track was being laid through them. The length of High Street tunnel was increased to 560 yards. The 971 yards of Withcall tunnel had produced many problems during its construction. Bad weather had continuously delayed work, the build up of water being so great in October 1874 that it resulted in a deluge which washed men out of the tunnel. In November of the same year there was a strike by the bricklayers, because their hands were so badly scalded by the wet lime that they could no longer hold a trowel. The death of Cornelius

> LOUTH & LINCOLN RAILWAY
> SECRETARY'S OFFICE
>
> Louth 13th June 1876
>
> Sir
>
> On behalf of the Louth & Lincoln Railway Company I hereby give notice that it is the intention of the Company to open their Railway constructed under "The Louth & Lincoln Railway Act 1866" and the Louth & Lincoln Railway Act 1872 and I shall be glad to receive necessary forms
>
> Your Obt Sert
> Fred. Sharpley
>
> The Assistant Secretary
> Railway Department
> Board of Trade
> Whitehall
> London.

Notice to the Board of Trade of "Intent to Open".
By kind permission of the Public Records Office, Kew, Reference MT6/168/1

Janaway in an accident involving a wagon in December was the culmination of the misfortunes relating to Withcall tunnel.

By March 1875 40 yards of Withcall tunnel remained to be lined and the GN were requested to proceed with the junctions at Louth and Bardney. The GN insisted on payments in cash or securities for the cost of installing the junctions, and proposed an annual charge of 10 per cent interest on the cost of installing a turntable at Louth, although this was later reduced to 5 per cent.

The opening of the line proceeded as follows: the 10 miles 49 chains from Bardney to South Willingham was opened to goods traffic on 9th November, 1874. This was extended a further 3 miles 5 chains to Donington-on-Bain by 27th September, 1875. The complete line was opened to goods traffic on the 26th June, 1876.

Opening to passenger traffic was delayed until 1st December, 1876. Board of Trade Inspector, Captain Tyler, inspected the line in June 1876, and would not recommend its opening until turntables had been installed at Louth and Bardney. A further inspection in October once again delayed opening because of defective workmanship at Bardney station. The turntable was being installed at Louth but the station still needed further modification for the operation of branch line trains.

Captain Tyler made a further inspection in November and was satisfied that his requirements had been met. The GN had built a new signal box at Bardney and a double line junction, spending £4,500 on the station. By July 1877 a new platform and alterations in the layout were completed.

A slight problem at Louth in the form of the Louth Volunteer Corps rifle range over which the line passed, briefly threatened the new passenger service. The GN warned the Rifle Corps that they were not prepared to risk the lives of their passengers, and that the service would be withdrawn unless that part of the line could be made safe. Needless to say such a guarantee was speedily forthcoming and rifles were pointed in another direction.

The original passenger service consisted of five trains each way on week days only. This was reduced to four trains by January 1877, only a month after services began. South Willingham was renamed South Willingham and Hainton, and Donnington dropped an "n" and became Donington. A siding was opened at Withcall in July 1878 followed, a month later, by a small station manned by a solitary station master with help from a youthful porter in the "Agricultural Season".

The summary of the complete 20 miles 79 chains of the Louth and Lincoln Railway would include the two tunnels at High Street (South

Willingham) and Withcall, several small bridges over waterways, five over-bridges; stations and sidings were at Kingthorpe, Wragby, East Barkwith, South Willingham, Donington-on-Bain, Withcall and Hallington.

The opening of the line did nothing to improve its prospects, in fact, the Louth and Lincoln problems were only just beginning. The imminent opening of the Louth to Mablethorpe Railway and the possibilities of extra traffic as a result did little to dispel the gloom of the early receipts which told a very different story to the wildly optimistic claims of the Prospectus. The 12 months July 1875 to June 1876 showed only £2,094 profit.

By July 1877 the Louth and Lincoln were again urging the GN to take over the line as quickly as possible. The GN, however, remained unmoved and refused to negotiate.

There was a degree of optimism about the statements made by the Directors at the beginning of 1878. They reported that the line had been taken over for maintenance by the GN. A poor harvest, general depression, and a failure to secure a share of the Grimsby traffic were used as excuses for the poor trading returns. Once again the Louth to Mablethorpe line was seen as a possible source of extra revenue.

June 1878 saw the company appealing to the GN again for financial help. The traffic from the Midlands anticipated by the Prospectus had failed to materialise. The Nottingham and Grantham trains continued to be routed via Boston and even when they were sent over the Louth and Lincoln rails the company received no cash returns from the journeys.

Another unsuccessful approach was made to the GN after a bad year in 1880. In 1881, however, negotiations were re-opened, and in May Mr Sharpley was appointed Permanent Receiver.

In August the GN expressed an interest in purchasing the line and offered a price of £200,000, this figure was slightly more than half the expenditure on the line. The Louth and Lincoln were on the rack and it was a case of getting the best offer to cut their losses. Considering that traffic receipts between 1876 and 1881 had never produced enough to pay the bank interest, it was no surprise that the offer was unanimously accepted by an Extraordinary Meeting of Shareholders on 20th December, 1881.

Royal Assent for the transfer was given in August 1882 and the Louth and Lincoln Railway Company passed into the possession of the Great Northern Railway Company on 30th June, 1883. An ignoble end to a bold but foolhardy piece of railway speculation.

Chapter Two

Operation of the Line

Of the stations at either end of the line, Louth was the more important. Starting life as the southern terminus, albeit briefly, of a line from New Holland on the 1st March, 1848, Louth became a through station some six months later when the East Lincolnshire line reached Firsby. The opening of the GNR main line, on 7th August, 1850, saw the line connected to London. The station at Louth had an overall roof spanning both up and down platforms. The main station building was constructed in an ornate mock Tudor style in contrast to the austere lines of most GNR stations and due, no doubt, to its construction by an independent company. Initially it had a footbridge situated at the southern end of the station and linking the two platforms. Later the platforms were linked by a subway which was a rare, but not unique, feature on the GNR system. Other facilities at Louth included a large brick-built goods shed, which replaced an earlier wooden one, five signal boxes, a sub-shed and turntable.

Bardney station opened on 17th October, 1848, and served a small town on the banks of the River Witham. With the opening of the Louth–Bardney branch the station was substantially modified. Lincoln to Boston trains were served by an island platform, branch line trains departing from a separate short platform to the east of the main line. Other facilities at Bardney included a goods shed and turntable. Leaving Bardney, Louth trains trundled over a level crossing, situated at the western end of the station, ran along the main line for a short distance before diverging in a northerly direction on to the branch.

Prior to 1923 locomotives working the Louth to Bardney line were supplied by 40A, Lincoln shed. After the grouping, locomotives were supplied by 40C, Louth shed. Closure of the Donington-on-Bain section of the line in September 1956, plus the onset of dieselisation saw the end of Louth shed in the same year.

Prior to the arrival of the Ivatt 4–4–2T 'C12s' and the 4–4–0 'D2' and 'D3s' in the twenties it is difficult to be certain about the different types of engines used on the branch before 1920. The large Sturrock 2–2–2 singles are known to have finished up in Lincolnshire but would not have been particularly suitable for the hilly stop-start nature of the Louth–Bardney. The later Sturrock 0–4–2Ts or the Stirling 0–4–2s were a more likely choice, as were the Stirling 0–4–4Ts, surplus in the London area after the appearance of the Ivatt 4–4–2T, 'C12s'.

After the grouping Louth's allocation of engines settled down to a more regular pattern, basically 'D2s', 'D3s', 'C12s' and ex-Great

Great Northern Railway Timetable of the 1880s.

Louth station seen from above.

H.L. Howe

An old postcard showing Louth station in its prime; note the station horse on the track.
H.C. Casserley Collection

A 1960 view of the impressive station building at Louth. *Mowat Collection*

A rail level view of Louth station photographed in 1954. *Lens of Sutton*

The trim South signal box at Louth, 1960. *Mowat Collection*

Louth looking south in 1965; the entrances to the subway can be seen on the platforms. *Mowat Collection*

Louth station looking north in the 1960s. *Author's Collection*

Louth South signal box. *Author's Collection*

Class 'C12s' both seen here on trains with No. 4548 in the Louth branch line bay platform with the Bardney line stock on 9th May, 1946.   *H.C. Casserley*

'C12' No. 4519 at Louth, still wearing its wartime abbreviated "NE" livery on 9th May, 1946.   *H.C. Casserley*

Louth station, seen from the north on 4th May, 1975.   *N.D. Mundy*

Louth shed in 1927: 4-4-0 No. 4307 and the last Stirling 2-4-0 No. 3814 stand outside.   *J.E. Kite*

'C12s' and stock at Louth; the main line is at the left, the branch bay at the right.
A.J. Wickens

"Dick", the Louth station horse "at home".
N.E. Stead

Class 'C12' No. 4013 (later No. 7352), one of the first batch of the class built by the GNR, at the north end of Louth station. The line to Grimsby is behind the engine. *N.E. Stead*

At Louth; driver Jack Ingoldmells, who was awarded the LNER medal for gallantry on the Bardney line, with fireman Charlie Cox and class 'C12' No. 4013. *N.E. Stead*

OPERATION OF THE LINE

Bradshaw's Timetable for October 1911.

Bradshaw's Timetable for 1922.

"THE BUFF BOOK" (LONDON TRADES DIRECTORY) IS IN EVERY IMPORTANT HOTEL. ASK FOR IT.

LNER Passenger Timetable for March 1938.

NOTES.

Bb Stops when required.
b Via Grantham. On Weds travel via Spalding.

MARCH, SPALDING, SLEAFORD, LINCOLN, DONCASTER, YORK, ETC.—continued.

DOWN—SUNDAYS.

4.24 p.m. Lincoln to Doncaster (Central).

UP—WEEKDAYS.

5.55 a.m. Doncaster (Central) to March.
8.5 a.m. Doncaster (Central) to March will not run Doncaster to Lincoln. Will start from Lincoln 9.20 a.m.
9.50 a.m. Doncaster (Central) to Lincoln.
11.10 a.m. Doncaster (Central) to March.
2.25 p.m. Doncaster (Central) to Lincoln.
3.44 p.m. Doncaster (Central) to Lincoln.
4.8 p.m. Lincoln to March.
6.5 p.m. Lincoln to March.
6.40 p.m. Doncaster (Central) to Lincoln.

UP—SUNDAYS.

4.30 p.m. Doncaster (Central) to Lincoln and Peterborough (North).

FIRSBY AND SKEGNESS.

WEEKDAYS.

Down.
8.40 a.m. Firsby to Skegness.
9.30 a.m. Leicester to Skegness (Saturdays only).
10.10 a.m. Nottingham to Skegness (Saturdays only).
10.21 a.m. Firsby to Skegness.
1.30 p.m. Firsby to Skegness will leave 1.10 p.m. and run 20 minutes earlier throughout.
4.15 p.m. Firsby to Skegness.
4.37 p.m. Firsby to Skegness (Saturdays only).
7.30 p.m. Firsby to Skegness.
7.46 p.m. Firsby to Skegness (Fridays only).

Up.
7.55 a.m. Skegness to Firsby.
9.30 a.m. Skegness to Firsby.
12.5 p.m. Skegness to Firsby.
3.0 p.m. Skegness to Leicester (Saturdays only).
3.20 p.m. Skegness to Firsby will leave 3.30 p.m. and run 10 minutes later throughout.
4.40 p.m. Skegness to Nottingham (Victoria) (Mondays and Saturdays only).
5.40 p.m. Skegness to Firsby.

FIRSBY AND SPILSBY.

WEEKDAYS.

Down.
8.47 a.m. Firsby to Spilsby.
10.22 a.m. Firsby to Spilsby.
1.30 p.m. Firsby to Spilsby will leave at 1.10 p.m. and run 20 minutes earlier throughout.
7.40 p.m. Firsby to Spilsby.

Up.
8.10 a.m. Spilsby to Firsby.
9.45 a.m. Spilsby to Firsby.
12.25 p.m. Spilsby to Firsby.
5.50 p.m. Spilsby to Firsby.

WOODHALL JUNCTION, WOODHALL SPA AND HORNCASTLE.

WEEKDAYS.

Down.
8.35 a.m. Woodhall Junction to Horncastle.
1.8 p.m. Woodhall Junction to Horncastle.
4.47 p.m. Woodhall Junction to Horncastle.
7.3 p.m. Woodhall Junction to Horncastle.

Up.
7.0 a.m. Horncastle to Woodhall Junction.
10.10 a.m. Horncastle to Woodhall Junction.
12.30 p.m. Horncastle to Woodhall Junction.
3.45 p.m. Horncastle to Woodhall Junction.
6.5 p.m. Horncastle to Woodhall Junction.

WOODHALL JUNCTION, LITTLE STEEPING AND FIRSBY (VIA CONINGSBY).

WEEKDAYS.

5.40 a.m. Woodhall Junction to Firsby.
7.25 a.m. Firsby to Woodhall Junction.
11.45 a.m. Woodhall Junction to Firsby.
1.25 p.m. Firsby to Woodhall Junction.
6.40 p.m. Woodhall Junction to Firsby.
4.20 p.m. Firsby to Woodhall Junction.

WILLOUGHBY, SUTTON-ON-SEA, MABLETHORPE AND LOUTH.

WEEKDAYS.

Down.		Up.	
	a.m.		a.m.
Willoughby to Mablethorpe.	8.50	Louth to Willoughby.	7.42
Nottingham (Victoria) to Mablethorpe (12.29 p.m. from Willoughby) (Sats. only).	10.10	Mablethorpe to Willoughby.	9.25
	p.m.		p.m.
Willoughby to Louth.	1.20	Mablethorpe to Nottingham (Vic.) (Mondays and Sats. only).	4.28
Willoughby to Mablethorpe (Sats. only).	4.53	Louth to Willoughby.	5.40
Willoughby to Louth (Sats. excepted) will run daily.	7.10		
Willoughby to Mablethorpe (Fridays only).	7.59		

LOUTH AND LINCOLN (VIA BARDNEY).

WEEKDAYS.

Down.		Up.	
	a.m.		a.m.
Louth to Bardney.	10.0	Bardney to Louth.	8.44
	p.m.		p.m.
Louth to Bardney.	4.33	Bardney to Louth	6.52

GRANTHAM AND LINCOLN.

WEEKDAYS.

Down.		Up.	
	a.m.		a.m.
Grantham to Lincoln.	7.15	Lincoln to Grantham.	7.80
Grantham to Lincoln.	11.26	Lincoln to Grantham.	10.28
	p.m.		p.m.
Grantham to Lincoln	2.50	Lincoln to Grantham.	4.5
Grantham to Lincoln.	4.12	Lincoln to Grantham.	4.20

LNER "Extra Services" Timetable for May 1926.

Central Railway 'J11s'. Other locomotives were shedded at Louth and some may have worked the branch. The infamous 'J21' of the early 1920 period, number 1806 and known as "that cow of an engine", was of early North Eastern Railway design. Built for the steep gradients of the Darlington–Penrith line it would have been ideal for the Louth–Bardney; 1806 finally gave up the ghost when its firebox fell out in Louth shed.

There was a Great Eastern Railway 'J69' No. 7352 at Louth in the 1930s. An ex-Manchester, Sheffield and Lincolnshire Railway Parker 'N5' was in evidence in the 1950s and certainly worked the line. There is photographic evidence of an ex-Great Central Railway 'D7' emerging from the Horncastle Road bridge. Ex-GCR 'D7s' Nos. 5684, 5701, 5703 and 5711 were shedded at Louth for varying periods during the early 1930s. Ex-GCR 'D9' No. 6029 was at Louth between 1938 and 1941. So although Louth's allocation rarely exceeded twelve locomotives at any one time they certainly comprised an interesting and cosmopolitan bunch of ancients.

A look at Louth's allocations for the 1920s through to the 1950s shows little basic change in the classes of locomotives.

At 31st Dec. 1922

'C2' 4–4–2T	1503	LNER 4503	
(later	1506	4506 later BR 67364	
LNER 'C12')	1513	4513	
'D1' 4–4–0	1383	LNER 'D2' 4383-2181	
'D2' 4–4–0	1304	LNER 'D3' 4304	
'E1' 2–4–0	814	LNER 3814	
	1000A	LNER 4000A	
Total 7			

At 31st Dec. 1927

'C12' 4–4–2T	4015	later 7354
	4019	7357
	4503	7361
	4506	7364
	4513	7370
	4525	7379
'D2' 4–4–0	4325	
	4383	later 2181
'D3' 4–4–0	4304	
	4307	later 2125
Total 10		

Spring 1934

'C12' 4–4–2T	4015	later 7354	
	4513	7370	
	4525	7379	
'D2' 4–4–0			
	4369	later 2172	
	4382		
	4383	later 2181	
	4397		
'D3' 4–4–0	4072		
	4314		
	4343	later 2135	
ex-GCR 'J11' 0–6–0	6008	later 4315	
Total 12			

1935

'C12' 4–4–2T	4015
(ex-GNR)	4525
'D2' 4–4–0	4325
(ex-GNR)	4369
	4382
	4383
	4397
'D3' 4–4–0	4072
(ex-GNR)	4314
	4343
'J11' 0–6–0	6008
(ex-GCR)	
'J69' 0–6–0	7352
(ex-GER)	
Total 12	

1950

'C12'	67352	pre-1946 4013	'D3'	2132	pre-1946 4317
	67364	4506	'J11'	64320	6043
	67379	4525		64328	6051
	67381	4528	'N5' 0-6-2T	69306	5766
	67383	4530	(ex-MS&LR)		
	67384	4531	Total 11		
	67398	4548			

Most of the work on the Louth–Bardney would be carried out by the 'C12s' and 'J11s'; 'C12s' worked the passenger services, the 'J11s' freight and occasionally passenger. Looking at the shed allocations it is interesting to note that 'C12' No. 4525, later 67379, was at Louth in 1927 and still there in 1950. This engine, in fact, pulled the last passenger train on the line in 1951. 'C12' No. 4013, later 67352, is perhaps interesting in that it was one of the first batch of eleven 'C12s'. These were distinguished from the rest of the class by having square cornered tanks and bunkers. No. 4015 of the 1927/1935 allocation is also one of this original batch.

Despite the large number of 'D2s' and 'D3s' at Louth in the 1935 list it is unlikely they worked the Bardney branch regularly, not being particularly suited for such terrain. They are more likely to have worked the Mablethorpe–Sutton-on-Sea loop and the East Lincolnshire line.

In the 1880s the Great Northern Railway ran six trains a day from Bardney:

	Down Trains			Up Trains		
	Bardney dep.	*Louth arr.*		*Louth dep.*	*Bardney arr.*
Goods	7.40am	10.20am	Pass.	8.05am	8.54am
Pass.	9.10am	10.01am	Cattle	10.10am (TO)	11.05am (TO)
Pass.	11.15am	12.06pm	Pass.	10.24am	11.13am
Goods	11.40am	1.35pm	Goods	12.00 nn (TX)	3.05pm (TX)
Pass.	4.20pm	5.16pm	Pass.	2.56pm	3.47pm
Pass.	7.03pm	7.45pm	Goods	4.20pm (SX)	6.50pm (SX)
			Pass.	5.35pm	6.26pm

(TO) = Tuesdays only, (TX) = Tuesdays excepted, (SX) = Saturdays excepted. There was no Sunday service.

1924 workings show departures from Louth at 7.45 and 10.00am, and 3.05 and 5.33pm, the second and third being shown as through to Lincoln. Departures from Bardney were at 8.44 and 11.29am, and 1.25, 3.02(FO), 4.20 and 6.57pm, the third being through from Lincoln. A goods service started from Louth at 8.40(MWFO) and returned from Bardney at 1.39pm. An additional goods service from

OPERATION OF THE LINE

LOUTH and BARDNEY

Miles		Week Days only						Miles			Week Days only		
		mrn	aft	aft						mrn	mrn	aft	
—	Louth .... dep	7 47	1235	3 57	..	..	..	—	52 London (King's C.)..dep	4 30	7818	1 25	..
3	Hallington	..	1241	Aa	..	..	..	—	52 Lincoln .... "	9 17	1 12	5 47	..
4½	Withcall	7 56	1246	4 8	..	..	..	—	Bardney .... dep	9 35	1 50	6 12	..
7½	Donington-on-Bain	8 5	1255	4 17	..	..	..	4	Kingthorpe	10 2	1 57	6 19	..
10½	South Willingham and	8 12	1 2	4 24	..	..	..	6	Wragby	10 8	2 3	6 25	..
12½	East Barkwith...[Hainton	8 16	1 6	4 28	..	..	..	9	East Barkwith...[Hainton	1013	2 8	6 30	..
15½	Wragby	8 22	1 13	4 34	..	..	..	10½	South Willingham and	1018	2 13	6 35	..
17½	Kingthorpe	8 26	1 17	4 38	..	..	..	13½	Donington-on-Bain	1025	2 21	6 42	..
21½	Bardney .... arr	8 34	1 24	4 46	..	..	..	16½	Withcall	1031	2 27	6 48	..
30½	Lincoln .... arr	8 56	2 3	5 13	..	..	..	18½	Hallington .... Aa	..	2 31	..	..
150½	52 London (King's C.) "	1215	555	958	..	..	..	21½	Louth .... arr	1041	2 37	6 57	..

Aa Stops when required.   B Via Lincoln.

LNER Passenger Timetable of May 1941.

LOUTH and BARDNEY

Miles		Week Days only				Miles			Week Days only		
		mrn	aft	aft				mrn	mrn	aft	
—	Louth .... dep	7 50	1243	3 57	..	—	52 London (King's C.)..dep	4 35	10 10	18 25	..
3	Hallington	..	1249	Aa	..	—	52 Lincoln .... "	9 20	1 20	5 56	..
4½	Withcall	..	1254	4 8	..	—	Bardney .... dep	9 35	1 50	6 15	..
7½	Donington-on-Bain	8 9	1 3	4 17	..	4	Kingthorpe	10 2	1 57	6 22	..
10½	South Willingham and	8 16	1 10	4 24	..	6	Wragby	10 8	2 3	6 28	..
12½	East Barkwith...[Hainton	8 20	1 14	4 28	..	9	East Barkwith...[Hainton	1013	2 8	6 33	..
15½	Wragby	8 26	1 21	4 34	..	10½	South Willingham and	1018	2 13	6 38	..
17½	Kingthorpe	8 30	1 25	4 38	..	13½	Donington-on-Bain	1025	2 21	6 45	..
21½	Bardney .... arr	8 38	1 32	4 46	..	16½	Withcall	1031	2 27	6 51	..
30½	Lincoln .... arr	8 59	2 3	5 11	..	18½	Hallington .... Aa	..	2 31	..	..
150½	52 London (King's C.) "	1212	5 18	9 23	..	21½	Louth .... arr	1041	2 37	7 1	..

Aa Stops when required.   B Via Lincoln.

LNER Passenger Timetable of October 1946.

LOUTH and BARDNEY

Miles		Week Days only				Miles			Week Days only		
		a.m	p.m	p.m				a.m	a.m	p.m	
—	Louth .... dep	7 48	1240	3 57	..	—	65 London (King's C.)..dep	4 0	8 30	18 30	..
3	Hallington	..	1246	Aa	..	—	65 Lincoln .... "	9 20	1 20	5 0	..
4½	Withcall	7 59	1251	4 8	..	—	Bardney .... dep	9 35	1 50	6 25	..
7½	Donington-on-Bain	8 7	1 0	4 17	..	4	Kingthorpe	10 2	1 57	6 32	..
10½	South Willingham and	8 14	1 7	4 24	..	6	Wragby	10 8	2 3	6 39	..
12½	East Barkwith...[Hainton	8 18	1 11	4 28	..	9	East Barkwith...[Hainton	1013	2 8	6 43	..
15½	Wragby	8 24	1 18	4 34	..	10½	South Willingham and	1018	2 13	6 48	..
17½	Kingthorpe	8 28	1 22	4 38	..	13½	Donington-on-Bain	1025	2 21	6 55	..
21½	Bardney .... arr	8 36	1 29	4 46	..	16½	Withcall	1031	2 27	7 1	..
30½	65 Lincoln .... arr	8 59	2 3	5 41	..	18½	Hallington .... Aa	..	2 31	..	..
150½	65 London (King's C.) "	1 20	5 25	9 50	..	21½	Louth .... arr	1041	2 37	7 13	..

Aa Stops when required.   B Via Lincoln.

British Railways Passenger Timetable of September 1949.

Table 57—FIRSBY AND SKEGNESS
Weekdays

10.42 a.m. Firsby to Skegness starts at 10.31 a.m. and runs 11 minutes earlier.
Additional train on Saturdays, 11.52 a.m. Firsby (9.0 a.m. Derby, Friargate), to Skegness (shown in June Notice) is discontinued.
1.0 p.m. Firsby to Skegness:—Connection departs King's Cross 7.18 a.m.
On Saturdays 4.45 p.m. Firsby to Skegness starts at 4.50 p.m. and runs five minutes later.
On Saturdays 9.40 p.m. Firsby to Skegness starts at 9.45 p.m. and runs five minutes later.
9.40 a.m. Skegness to Firsby starts at 9.39 a.m., departs Wainfleet 9.49, calls also at Thorpe Culvert 9.53, and arrives Firsby 9.58 a.m.
Additional train on Saturdays, 2.30 p.m. Skegness to Firsby and Derby (Friargate) (shown in June Notice), is discontinued.

Table 58—WILLOUGHBY, SUTTON-ON-SEA, MABLETHORPE, AND LOUTH
Weekdays

Additional train on Sats., 12.6 p.m. Willoughby to Mablethorpe (shown in June Notice) is discontinued.
Additional train on Sats., 2.15 p.m. Mablethorpe to Willoughby (shown in June Notice), is discontinued.
2.15 p.m. Louth to Willoughby starts at 1E45 and 1S47 p.m. and is retimed as follows (cols. 1 and 2):—
An additional train runs as follows (col. 3):—

		1 E p.m.	2 S p.m.	3 p.m.
Louth	dep.	1 45	1 47	3 25
Grimoldby	,,	1 54	1 54	3 34
Saltfleetby	,,	2 2	2 2	3 42
Theddlethorpe	,,	2 7	2 7	3 47
Mablethorpe	arr.	2 13	2 18	3 53
,,	dep.	2 15	2 23	3 55
Sutton-on-Sea	arr.	2 20	2 28	4 0
,,	dep.	2 22	2 33	4 2
Mumby Road	,,	2 30	2 41	4 10
Willoughby	arr.	2 36	2 47	4 16

E Except Saturdays. S Saturdays only.

Table 59—WOODHALL JUNCTION, CONINGSBY, AND FIRSBY
Weekdays

1.4 p.m. Firsby to Woodhall Junction:—Connection departs King's Cross 7.18 a.m.

Table 60—LOUTH AND BARDNEY
Weekdays

Additional train departs Louth 12.35 p.m., Hallington 12.41, Withcall 12.46, Donington-on-Bain 12.55, South Willingham and Hainton 1.2, East Barkwith 1.6, Wragby 1.13, Kingthorpe 1.17, and arrives Bardney 1.24 p.m.
3.57 p.m. Louth to Bardney:—Connection departs King's Cross 7.18 a.m.
Additional train departs Bardney 1.45 p.m., Kingthorpe 1.52, Wragby 1.58, East Barkwith 2.3, South Willingham and Hainton 2.8, Donington-on-Bain 2.16, Withcall 2.22, Hallington 2.26, and arrives Louth 2.32 p.m.

SUPPLEMENT
TO
TIME TABLES

dated 1st APRIL to 30th JUNE, 1940

(EXCLUDING LONDON SUBURBAN SERVICES)

LNER

1st JULY, 1940

Superseding Supplements dated 1st May and 1st June, 1940

LNER Timetable Supplement for July 1940.

Louth to Bardney only left at 3.30pm(FX), and 3.35(FO) conveying cattle from Louth market to Lincoln.

Louth engine diagram 9 worked the 7.45am, 10.00am and 3.05pm departures, returning from Bardney with the 8.44am, 11.29am and 4.20pm respectively. The 11.29am train with the same engine departed from Louth for Grimsby at 12.20pm, arriving at 12.50pm and returning to Louth at 1.05pm. Similarly the 4.20pm departure from Bardney also worked through to Grimsby, departing from Louth at 5.30pm and arriving back at 7.25pm. This train then formed the 7.33pm to Sutton-on-Sea where it arrived at 8.10pm and left at 8.40pm, arriving back at Louth at 9.17pm. The 1.25pm Bardney to Louth service, which left Lincoln at 12.55pm, was worked by a Lincoln engine and crew, who worked back on the 3.30pm or 3.35pm goods. They finally took the 6.28pm Bardney to Lincoln passenger train home.

The 5.33pm from Louth, was included in Louth shed's number 4 diagram and had worked several other duties to Willoughby and Grimsby during the day. An engine ran light to Bardney on Fridays to work the 3.28pm back to Louth. The 8.40am goods was number 6 diagram, doing no more work after returning to Louth at 5.05pm.

In the 1930s a passenger train would leave Louth for Bardney at 7.42am arriving at 8.30am. This would be followed at 8.05am by a pick-up goods train which proceeded to Donington-on-Bain where it waited for the 9.10am from Bardney to pass through the station. It then moved on to Wragby, where it paused for the 9.50am from Louth to pass before continuing to Bardney.

The only connection with Grimsby was the 11.40am from Bardney arriving at Louth at 12.40pm. A train from the Mablethorpe branch would also connect with the Grimsby train at this time.

Throughout World War II three trains a day, weekdays only, were run. The dinner time up train left Louth at 12.35pm and the last down train left Bardney at 6.12pm.

During the last years of its operation the passenger service comprised of three trains each way, Mondays to Saturdays. There was also a goods train on each of those days although this did not always run on Saturdays. There was no Sunday service. This arrangement was not changed much after this until the final closing. The last down train from Bardney was scheduled to arrive at Louth at 7.13, before the Kings Cross to Cleethorpes express which arrived at 7.21pm. In September 1950, however, the latter was retimed to reach Louth at 7.15pm and the Bardney train was scheduled to reach Louth at 7.21pm. This meant that the train from Bardney was held at Withcall until the express had passed the junction. Very often, when the express was late the branch line train was allowed to reach Louth first.

From June 1951 the dinner time train was retimed to leave Louth at 12.25pm and run 15 minutes earlier all the way. For the last eight weeks of operation from the 10th September to 3rd November, 1951 the 12.25pm up train and the 1.50pm down train ran on Fridays and Saturdays only. The goods train timing for 10th June, 1951 onwards shows departure from Louth at 8.05am calling at Hallington and Withcall if required. Arrival at Donington-on-Bain was at 8.50am and departure at 9.05am. Calls at South Willingham and East Barkwith were at 9.21am and 9.50am respectively. The train arrived at Wragby at 10.00am and departed at 10.50am. Kingthorpe was reached at 11.00am and Bardney at 11.13am. The return working saw the train leave Bardney at 12.05pm, stop at Kingthorpe if required and arrive at Wragby at 12.27pm. Leaving here at 1.25pm it reached Donington-on-Bain at 2.00pm, stopping on the way at East Barkwith and South Willingham if required. Departure from Donington-on-Bain was at 2.40pm. Calls at Withcall and Hallington were made, if required, and arrival at Louth was at 3.20pm.

The up goods crossed with the 9.55am down passenger train at Wragby. In the reverse direction the down goods was scheduled to pass the 12.25pm up passenger train at Wragby. This, however, rarely happened as usually the goods ran early and went through as far as Donington-on-Bain, passing the passenger train there.

After the withdrawal of the passenger service in 1951 the service was reduced to two goods trains a day and any timetable existed in name only. Dr I.C. Allen recalls 'J11' No. 64320, pulling three trucks and a guards van, appearing from under London Road bridge and stopping for some time while the crew enjoyed watching a game of cricket in progress on Louth Cricket Club's ground.

The outward journey from Louth to Bardney was hard work for the engine crew. According to Mr Bullivant, who fired on the line during World War II, a full head of steam was essential out of Louth. The coal was broken down into small walnut-sized pieces and placed in the corners and back of the firebox, none under the door. A good driver would avoid moving the coal too far forward in the firebox. In wet conditions the sanders would be operating most of the way to Willingham tunnel on the outward journey. Withcall tunnel was a particular problem because of the steep climb to, and inside, the tunnel. In wet or greasy conditions trains often had to make a couple of attempts to get through and, on some occasions, goods trains had to be split to negotiate the greasy lines. The smoke inside the tunnel would sometimes force the engine crew onto the cab floor with a wet

Ex-GCR 'N5' class No. 69306 at Louth on the 7.48 am from Grimsby to Bardney on 1st June, 1951.
M. Black

Louth's two ex-GCR Class 'J11s' Nos. 64320 and 64328 in Louth yard.
N.E. Stead

The 3.57 pm from Louth to Bardney passing Hallington home signal on 6th June, 1951, hauled by 'C12' class No. 67379. *M. Black*

Hallington signal box, seen in April 1951. Note the abbreviated buffer stops on the loop siding. *M. Black*

A charming photograph of Hallington signal box taken in the 1890s.
Peter Chapman Collection

Class 'C12' No. 7352 stops at Withcall with the 9.55 am Bardney–Louth on 10th June, 1947. *W.A. Camwell*

A view of Hallington station looking east in the 1890s with the station staff and family in attendance. *Peter Chapman Collection*

Withcall station, seen in April 1983. *A.J. Ludlam*

(*Below*) The late Tom Ayre (in overalls), who helped a great deal with this book, seen here outside Withcall signal box; July 1939.
Author's Collection

(*Left*) Withcall signal box, July 1939.
B. Abbott

In April 1951 class 'C12' pauses at Withcall station with an up passenger train.
M. Black

The 12.40 pm from Louth to Bardney at Withcall on 15th June, 1951, hauled by ex-GCR 'N5' class No. 69306.
M. Black

Donington-on-Bain station (April 1951). *C. Bremner-Smith*

Donington-on-Bain in the early twenties: station master Margisson, the Rev. Jollye of Withcall stand in the foreground; clerk A.E. Green and porter H. Bosnell remain on the platform. *Author's Collection*

Donington-on-Bain station building as it was in April 1983. *A.J. Ludlam*

An RCTS railtour stopped at Donington-on-Bain on 16th May, 1954. The road overbridge is now filled in. *H.B. Priestley*

15 GREAT NORTHERN SECTION.
WEEK DAYS.
LOUTH AND MABLETHORPE BRANCH.

		a.m.	a.m.	a.m.	p.m.	p.m.	p.m.	p.m.
Willoughby	dep.		11 20			7 30	9 53	5 35
Mumby Road	,,		11 28			7 38	10 2	5 44
Sutton-on-Sea	,,		1 35			7 45	10 10	5 52
Mablethorpe	,,		11 43			7 54	10 15	5 57
Theddlethorpe	,,		11 49			7 59	10 23	6 11
Saltfleetby	,,		11 53			8 4	10 28	6 14
Grimoldby	,,		12 1			8 12	10 36	6 21
Louth	arr.		12 10			8 20	10 43	6 27

SKEGNESS BRANCH.

		a.m.	a.m.	a.m.	p.m.	p.m.	p.m.
Firsby	dep.		8 35	10 30	1 10		
Thorpe Culvert	,,		8 41	10 36	1 16		
Wainfleet	,,	7 20	8 46	10 31	1 21		
Havenhouse	,,		8 51	10 36	1 26		
Seacroft	,,		8 57	10 42	1 32	2 10	
Skegness	arr.	7 30	9 10	10 45	1 35		

HORNCASTLE BRANCH.

		a.m.	a.m.	a.m.	p.m.	p.m.
Woodhall Jct.	dep.	8 40	9 55	11 20	1 5	5 15
Spa.	,,	8 45	10 0	11 25	1 15	5 21
Horncastle	arr.	8 55	10 10	11 36	1 20	5 30

LOUTH AND BARDNEY BRANCH.

		a.m.	p.m.
Bardney	dep.	8 50	4 30
Kingthorpe	,,	9 0	4 37
Wragby	,,	9 8	4 44
S. Barkwith	,,	9 13	4 44
S. Willingham	,,	9 23	4 54
Donington-on-Bain	,,	9 29	5 0
Withcall	,,	9 33	5 4
Hallington	,,		5 11
Louth	arr.	9 40	5 11

CONINGSBY BRANCH.

		a.m.	p.m.
Lincoln	dep.	7 0	2 36
Bardney	,,	7 19	2 53
Woodhall Junction	,,	7 33	3 5
Coningsby	,,	7 40	3 13
Tumby Woodside	,,	7 45	3 18
N. Bolingbroke	,,	7 50	3 23
Stickney	,,	7 56	3 35
Midville	,,	8 2	3 43
Little Steeping	,,	8 10	3 49
Firsby	arr.	8 18	

SPILSBY BRANCH.

		a.m.	a.m.	p.m.	p.m.
Firsby	dep.	7 10	10 47	5 8	10 56
Halton Holgate	,,	7 16	10 55	5 14	11 4
Spilsby	arr.	7 31	11 0	5 20	11 9

LONDON & NORTH EASTERN RAILWAY.

CANCELLATION

OF

CHEAP FARE FACILITIES

On and from Monday, 28th January, the issue of all Cheap Fare Facilities, with the exception of the following, will be withdrawn until further notice:—

WORKMEN'S TICKETS

COMMERCIAL TRAVELLERS

THEATRICALS

MUSIC HALL ARTISTES

SHIPWRECKED MARINERS

NAVAL

MILITARY & POLICE

LNER "Cancellation of Cheap Fares" pamphlet, showing trains affected.

handkerchief covering their faces to combat the fumes.

Owing to a generally falling gradient, the return journey from Bardney to Louth was a much easier trip for the driver and fireman.

Passenger stock varied little over the years and usually consisted of a pair of ancient carriages pulled by a 'C12'. Ironically the Bardney branch carriages were replaced by the Mablethorpe branch stock for the final passenger trip, the Mablethorpe stock being deemed more comfortable for the passengers! The 'J11' "Pom Poms" usually handled the goods traffic on the line. There was a restriction of 11 mineral wagons between Louth and Donington-on-Bain because of heavy gradients between the two stations. During World War II a train carrying incendiary bombs would consist of between 30 and 40 wagons. Farm produce constituted a large part of the freight traffic, sugar beet for the factory at Bardney being a major commodity.

Especially during World War II, a tender or bunker full of coal was a valuable asset and was often used as a means of barter for all manner of local produce. That it was often difficult to move on the footplate, because of "exchanged goods", is frequently enough reported for one to draw the conclusion that the "lump of coal for a dozen eggs" trade was alive and well on the Bardney branch.

Tom Ayre remembered some of the drivers who worked at Louth: first link men Sid Welbourne and George Smalley; branch line men included Charlie Smith, Sid Gill, Fred Crosskill, Sol Janney, who reputedly took a passenger train from Louth to Grimsby in 16 minutes! "Cracker" Dowse, Johnny Broddle, "Jegger" Smith, "Bumper" Cartwright, so named because of his role as a stopper full-back in Louth's Great Northern Railway football team.

Two methods of single line operating were used on the Louth–Bardney line. The original method of Staff and Paper Ticket was replaced in the early 1930s by an unusual, although not unique, system known as the Metal Tickets in a Staff system. This type of working was installed between Louth South and Donington-on-Bain, and between Donington-on-Bain and Wragby. There were electrically operated instruments at Louth South, Donington-on-Bain and Wragby. When the Staff at one end of the section was free to be removed from the instrument, the Staff at the other end was locked up so that it could not be shown or handed to the engine crew. The metal tickets were so controlled that they could not be extracted from the instrument unless the relative Staff was free. Each train proceeded on the authority of a metal ticket only after the driver had been shown the Staff, except when it was necessary for a train to enter the section and return to the signal box at which it entered the section. In this instance the driver or fireman would be handed the

Staff. The same principles used on the two sections of the Bardney line were also used on the two branches from Bury St Edmunds, and the Staffs and metal tickets off these lines are at the National Railway Museum at York.

A rationalisation scheme carried out at the beginning of World War II brought the control of stations along the line under the control of two station masters. Mr Jones at Donington-on-Bain was also responsible for Hallington, Withcall and South Willingham. Mr Paul at Wragby controlled East Barkwith and Kingthorpe halt.

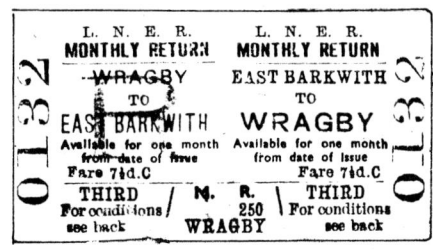

231.—LOUTH AND LINCOLN.

Incorporated by 29 and 30 Vic., cap. 344 (6th August, 1866), to construct a railway from Louth to the Great Northern Loop line at Lincoln. Length, 21 miles. Capital, 250,000*l.* in 10*l.* shares, and 83,000*l.* on loan. Arrangements with Great Northern.

No. of Directors—5; minimum, 3; quorum, 3 and 2. *Qualification*, 250*l.*

DIRECTORS:

Edward Heneage, Esq., 5, Grosvenor Crescent, S.W.
Henry Chaplin, Esq., M.P., Blankney, Lincolnshire.

William Thomas Kime, Esq.
Robert Norfolk, Esq.
Charles Edward Lucas, Esq.

Bradshaw's Shareholders' Manual of 1870.

Chapter Three

The Line at Work

The *Lincolnshire Chronicle* described the line's opening in its issue of Friday 8th December, 1876:

> Louth: After many disappointments and weary anticipation, the Directors and Shareholders of the Louth and Lincoln Railway may at length be congratulated on the opening of what promises to be a useful line. The first public passenger train left Louth for Bardney on Friday morning last at eight o'clock, several of our townsmen availed themselves of the opportunity of making a direct and speedy journey to Lincoln market. According to present arrangements four trains run daily each way with a fifth on Fridays so that ample accommodation is afforded for the passenger traffic of the district. Those who have travelled by the new line speak in high terms of its construction and of the ease and steadiness with which the coaches travel along it. Those who visit Louth by this line will be agreeably surprised to find that it passes through some really picturesque scenery with features as good as any to be found in the country.

A look at *Kelly's Directory* of 1905 gives an indication of some of the goods carried by the railway. As well as the local coal merchants based at most stations, there were:

> WRAGBY William Mawer and Son, miller and corn and cattle cake merchant.
> EAST BARKWITH Alf Duckering, nursery man, seedsman, bonecrusher and chemical manure manufacturer.
> James Foster, timber merchant, agricultural implement maker and wheelwright.
> DONINGTON-ON-BAIN John Brocklebank, brick and tile maker, coal merchant and white sand pits.
> SOUTH WILLINGHAM had its miller.

As well as transporting cattle, sheep and other livestock, the line looked after the needs of agriculture in general: Peruvian guano to be spread on the land, rock salt for cattle licks and locust beans for cattle slabs.

James Dales lived at Withcall in the 1920s. His father worked for the company. There was a staff of seven based at Withcall at that time, four platelayers, a station master, signalman and porter. A platelayer earned in the region of 19/- a week with one shilling or one and sixpence deducted for rent on a company tied house. These houses were well built and certainly above the average of most rural dwellings of the day despite having no running water, bathroom, gas or electricity. Mr Dales recalled an engine driver named John Portess working the branch at that time, his father of the same name was a ganger on the line and a local lay preacher. Mr Dales' father used to

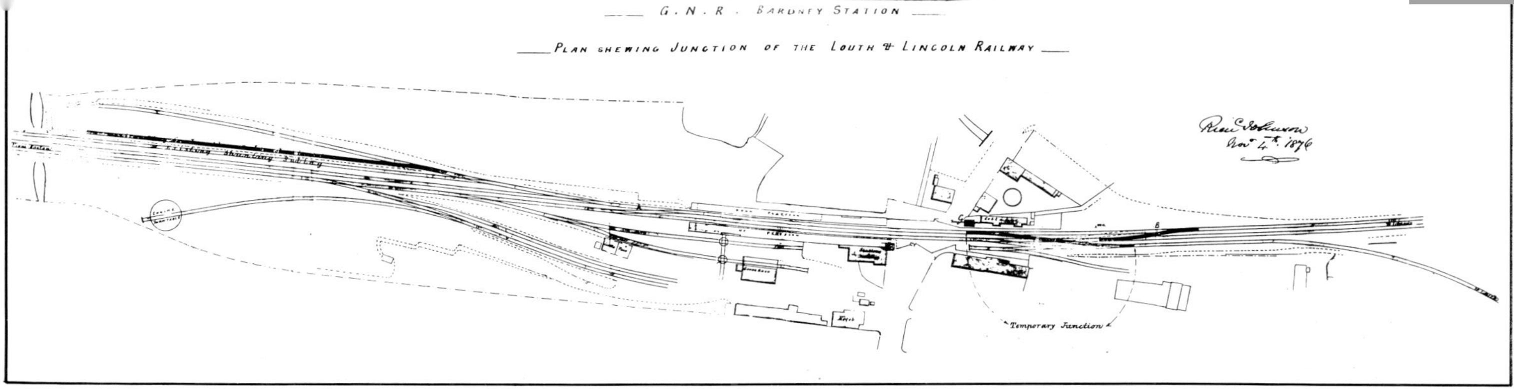

The 1876 track plan of Bardney station showing the Louth line on the far right.

The trackplan in the early 1900s.

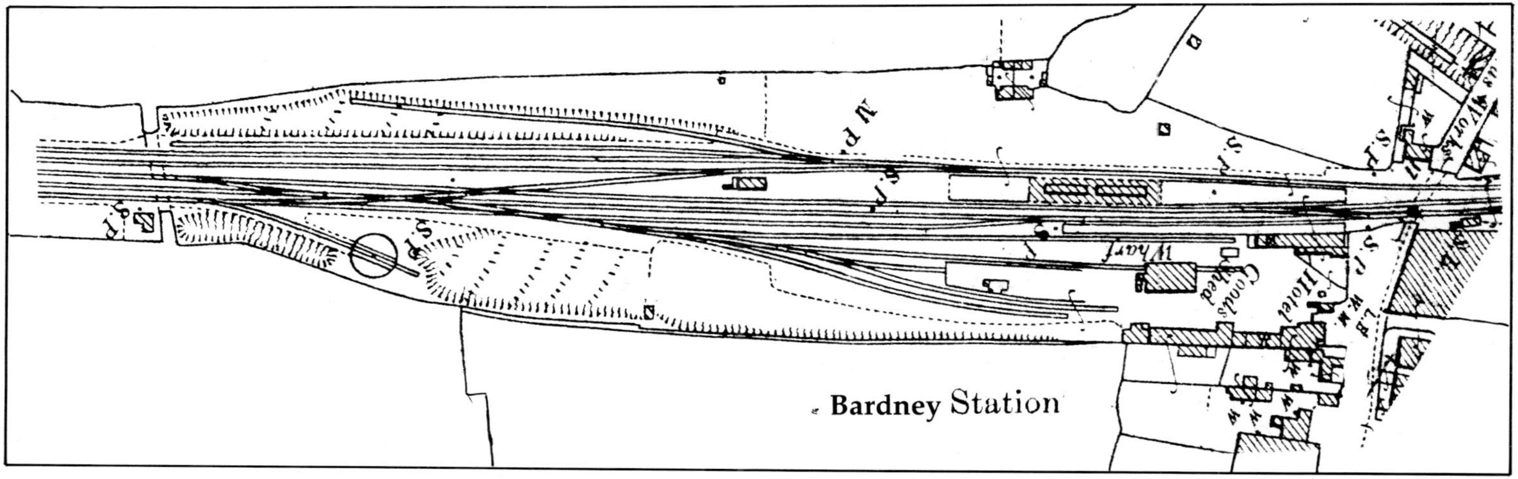

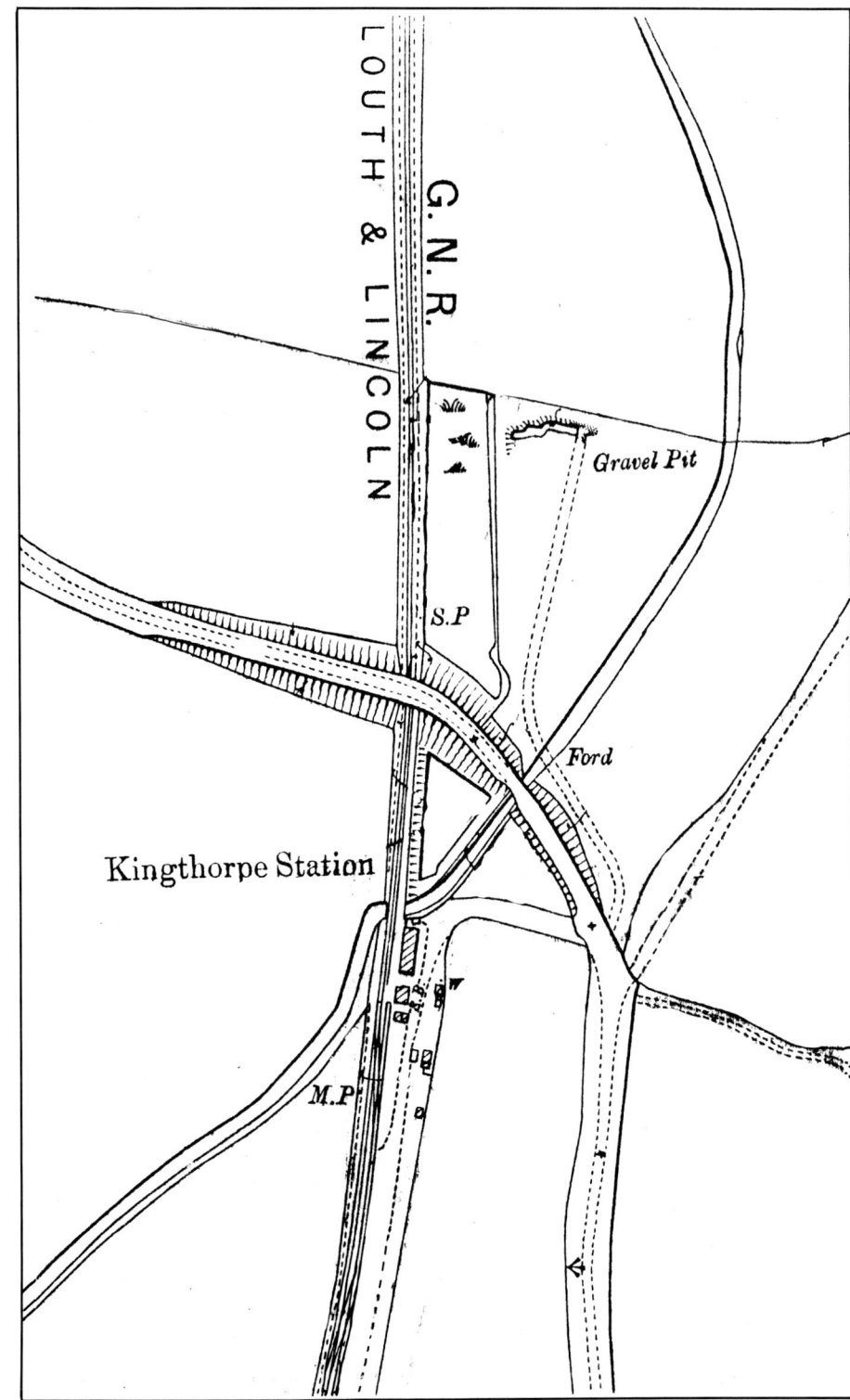

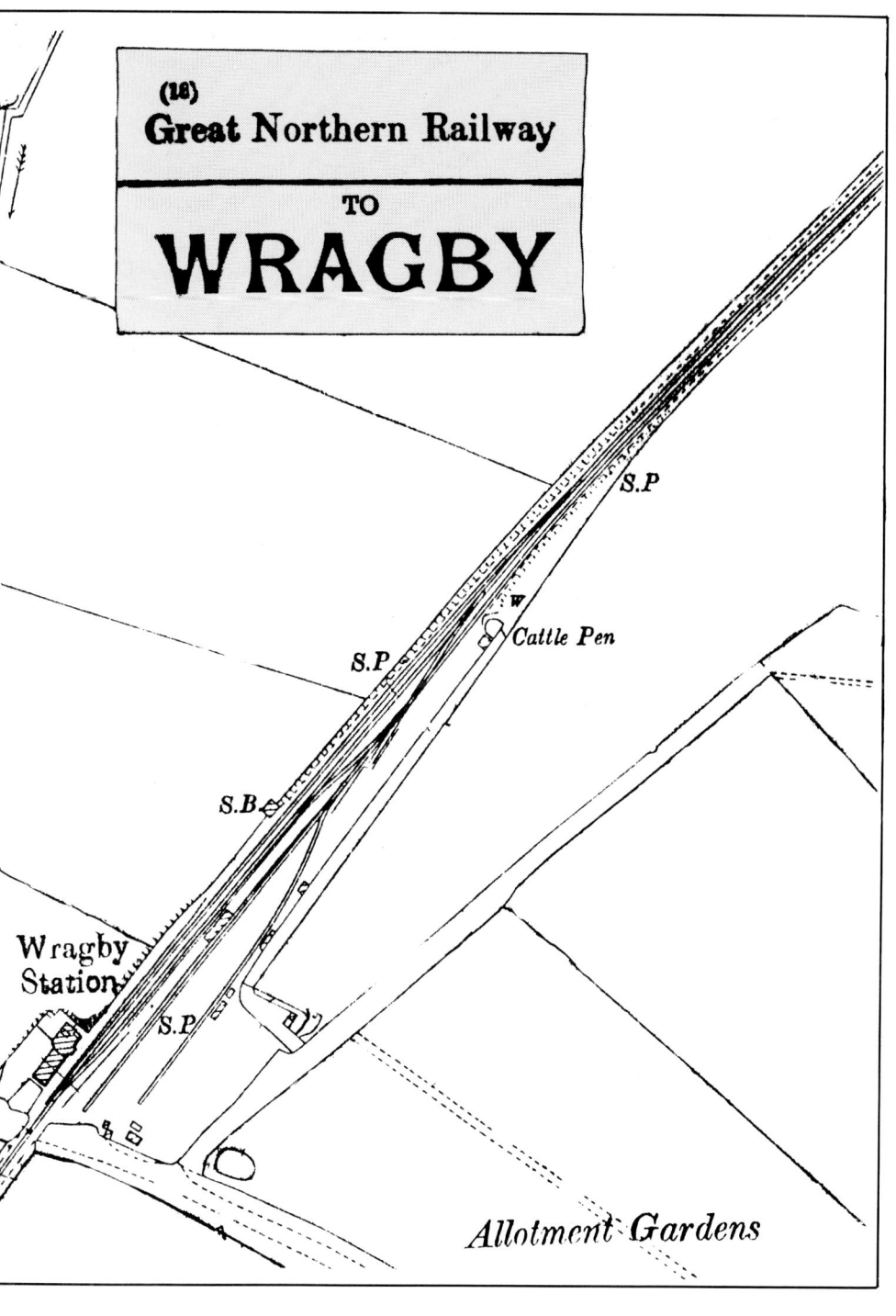

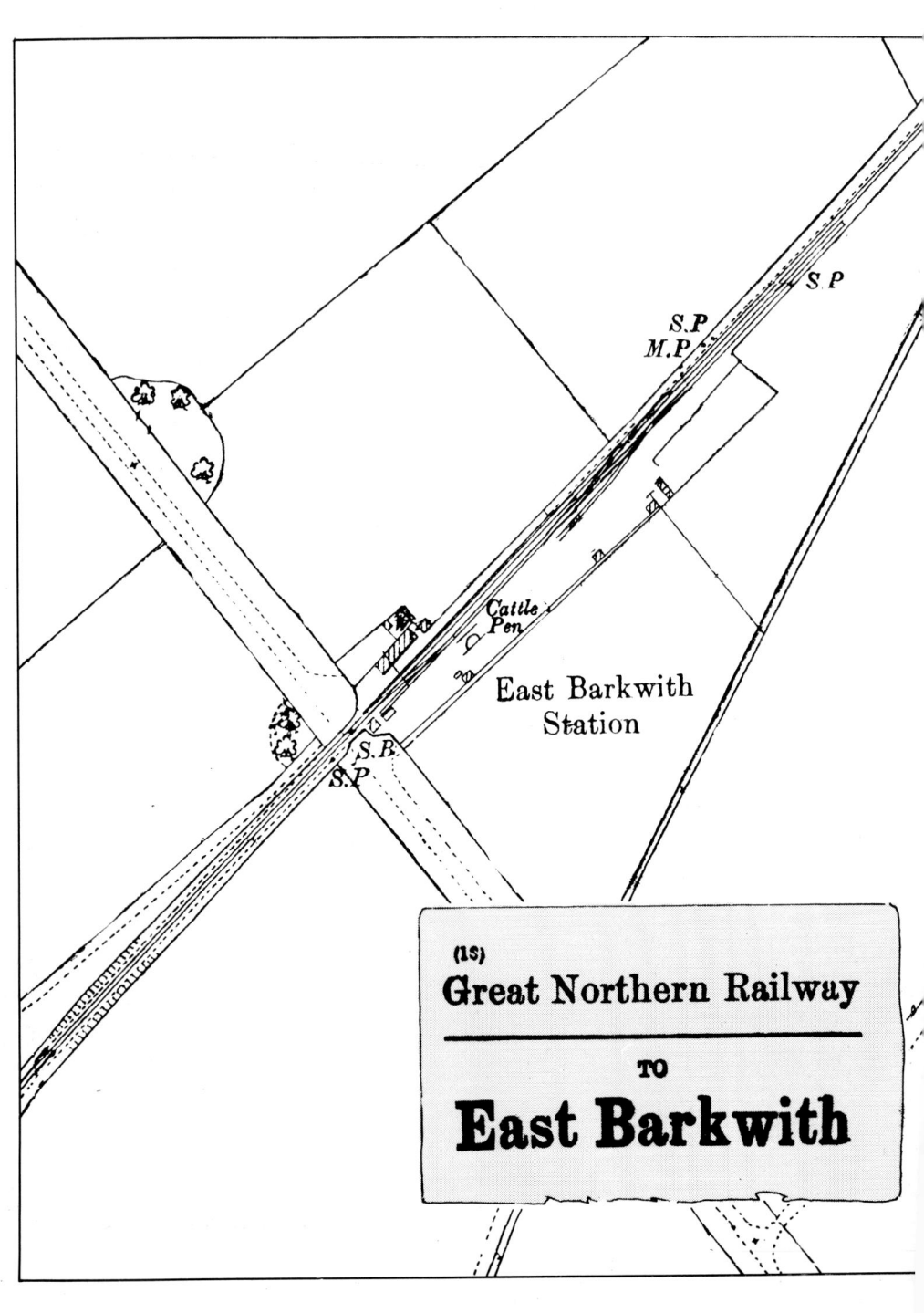

Class 'J11' 0–6–0 No. 64323 passes Donington-on-Bain with a down freight, April 1951.
M. Black

A class 'J11' on a passenger train for Bardney at Donington-on-Bain.
C. Bremner-Smith

(*Left*) Donington-on-Bain signal box, July 1939.   *B. Abbott*

(*Right*) Porter H. Bosnell and clerk A.E. Green at Donington-on-Bain in 1930.   *Author's Collection*

Class 'C12' No. 67394 passes the 'up' home signal at Donington-Bain; note the post on the opposite side of the line which helps to support the rather tall signal in this exposed location.   *M. Black*

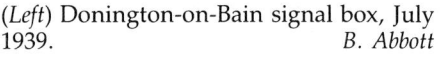

South Willingham and Hainton station looking west, June 1951. *M. Black*

A 'C12' east of South Willingham on a Bardney to Louth train.
C. Bremner-Smith

Although photographed in 1951, LNER signs are still visible at East Barkwith station.
M. Black

East Barkwith station in 1951.
M. Black

The staff at Wragby station pose for the photographer; note the pathway from the level crossing to the up platform (there was no footbridge). *Lens of Sutton*

Wragby in GNR days (the poster boards under the large "Wragby" sign are headed by that company's name). *Lens of Sutton*

A busy scene at Wragby in GNR days. *Author's Collection*

Wragby station looking east, seen on 29th September, 1956. By this time the line was only open for freight between Bardney and Donington but observe that full signalling still exists at Wragby. *H.B. Priestley*

A westward-looking view of Wragby Station (June 1951). *M. Black*

This view of Wragby station looking east shows the long crossing loops that were available here (June 1951). *M. Black*

A Louth–Bardney fast train nearing Wragby headed by 4-4-0 No. 4343. *J.E. Kite*

Class 'J6' No. 64219 at Wragby in October 1959. *M. Black*

Wragby station yard as it was in June 1961. *M. Black*

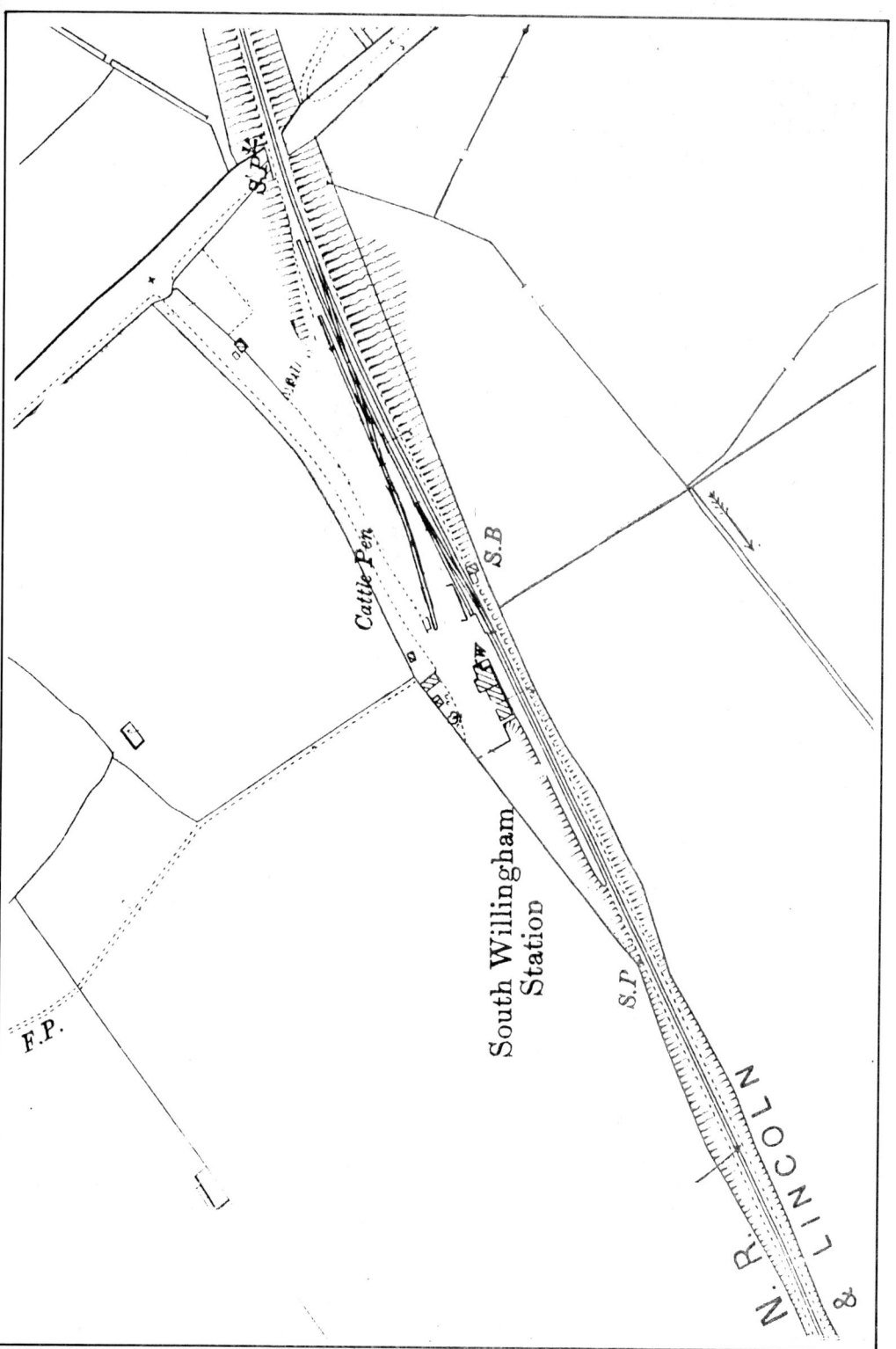

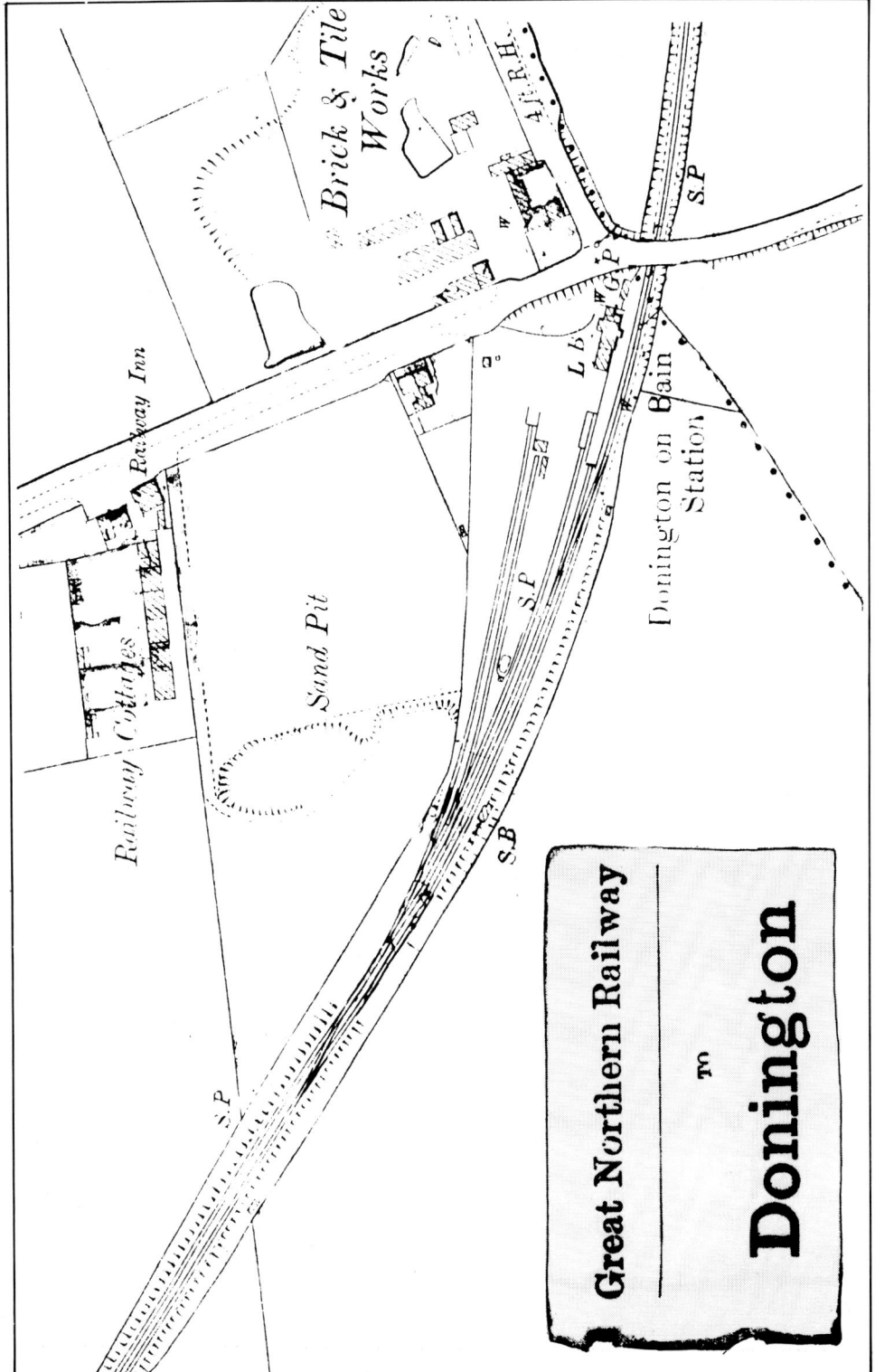

Moat
W
S.P
S.P
Withcall Station
S.B
W
(18)
Great Northern Railway
TO
WITHCALL

Hallington
Station
F.P.
S.B.
Cattle Pen
C.Tk.D.

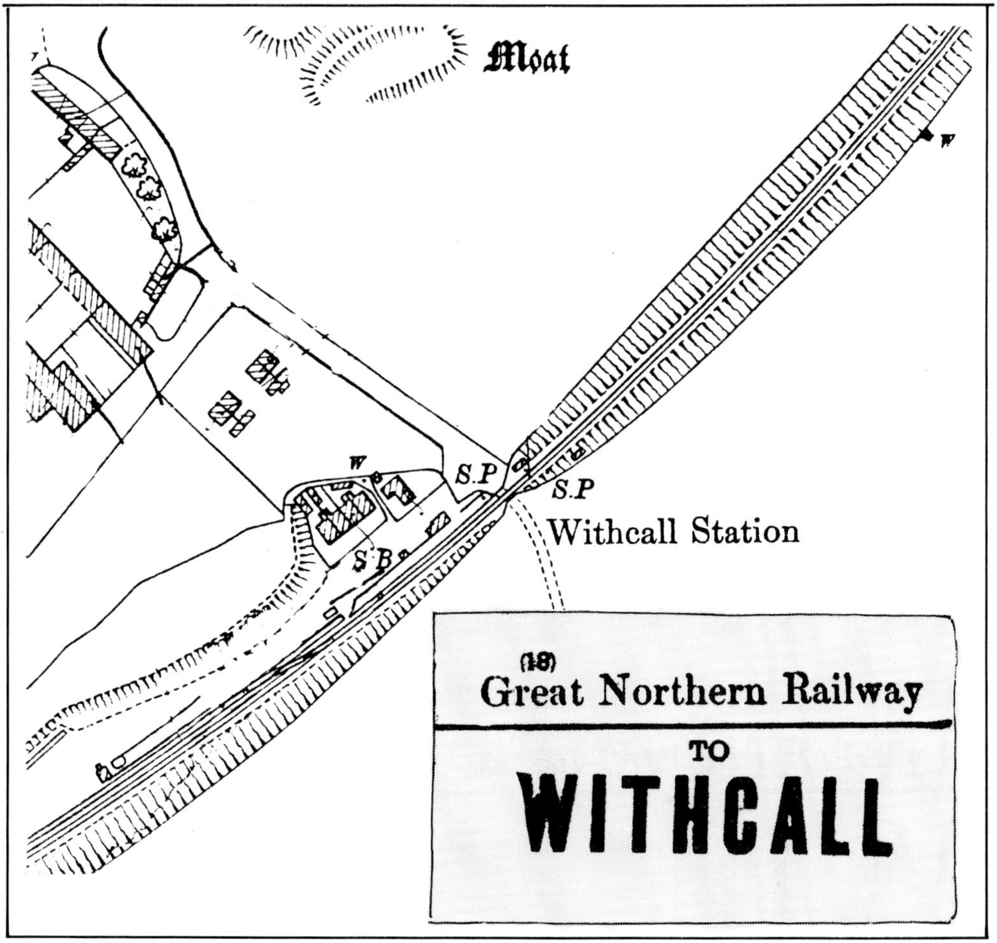

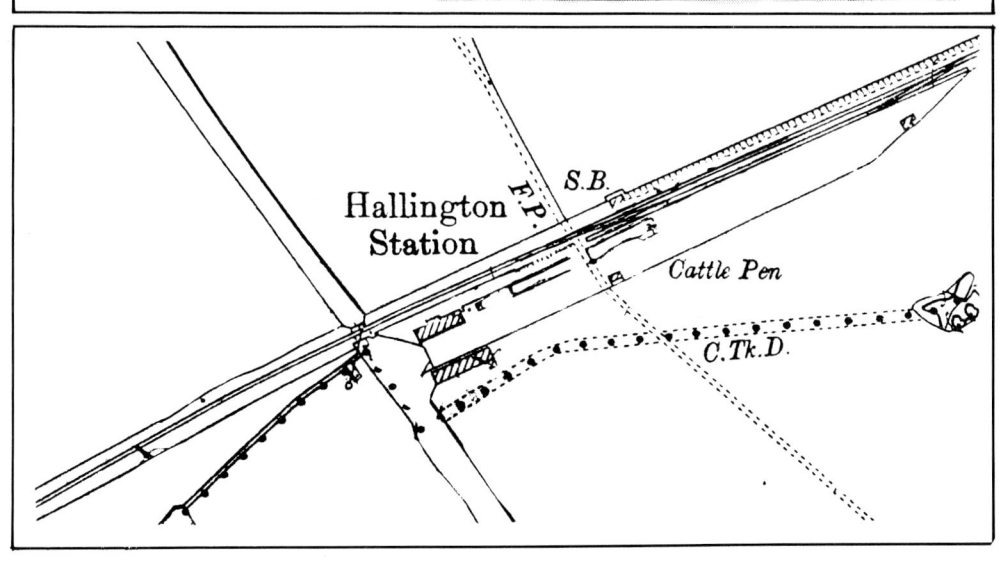

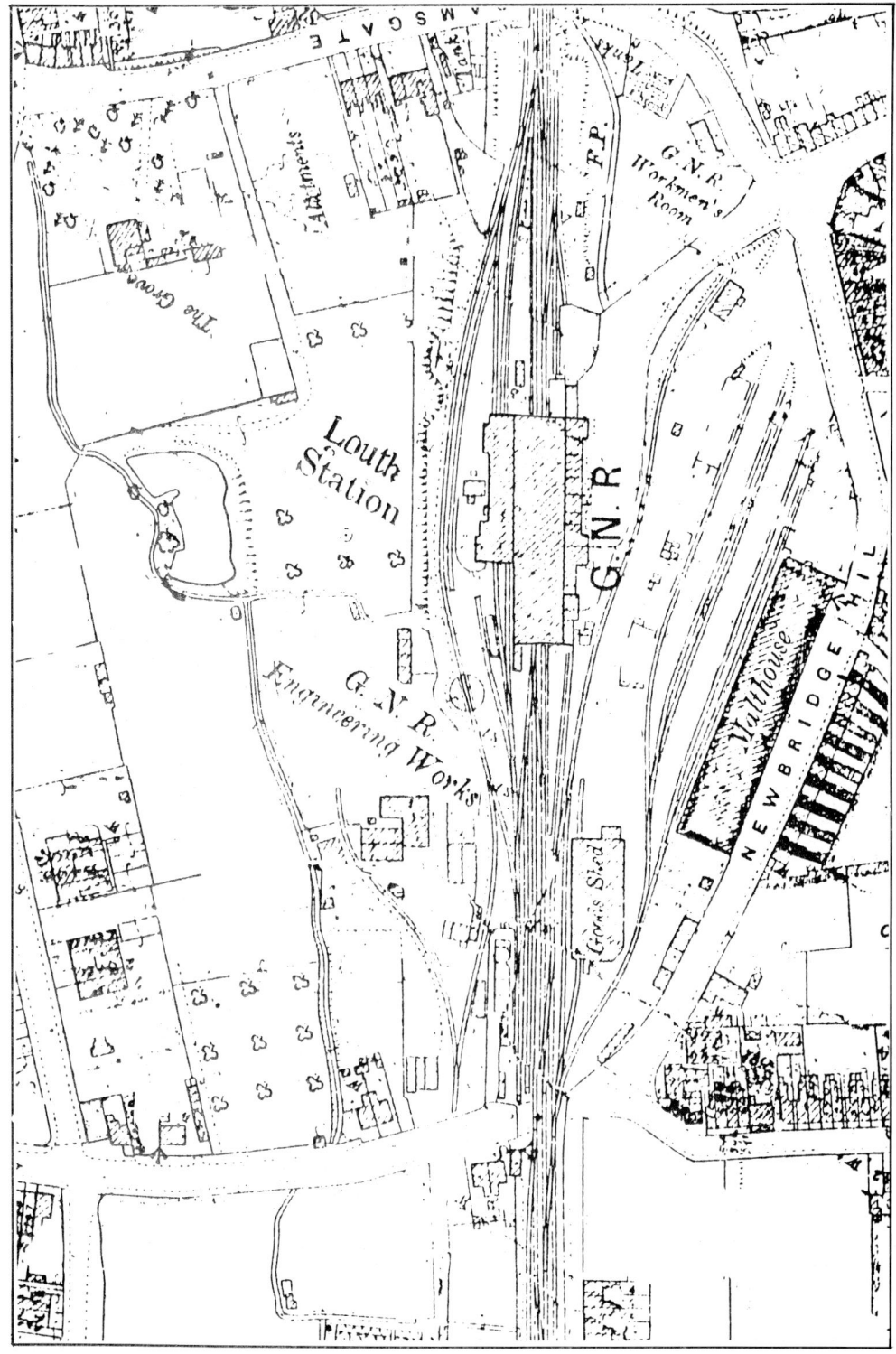

work the length from Willingham to Louth, including both tunnels. Walking his length in 1947 Mr Dales senior found a snow covered ball in the snow; he kicked it only to discover it was a head; the body was later found near Withcall tunnel. An unusual feature of Withcall tunnel was its lack of manholes, or wall recesses, in the tunnel side walls, where workmen could stand while trains passed. In Withcall they had to press themselves against the wall or squatted down until the train passed. This oversight on the part of the designer was rectified in Willingham tunnel which was supplied with manholes.

The period between the two World Wars was the era of the branch line and the Louth-Bardney railway enjoyed its happiest times.

The railway had become an established part of rural life. Before telephones began being installed in the area during the middle 1920s the station was the focal point for emergency calls to doctors and hospitals. The messages were tapped out by the signal man over the telegraph to the signal box at Louth.

The busiest days for passengers were Wednesdays and Saturdays with most passengers travelling to Louth market. The women would often gather at the stations to exchange gossip an hour or more before the train was due. The chatter would continue in the long open carriage of the train known as the "Dining Car" because of its frequent use for breastfeeding babies.

When the local springs dried up the railway would supply a tender of water, which would be left in a siding for the use of railway employees. Later, drinking water for most stations on the line was supplied from the Donington station tap, itself served by a 3 inch bore pipe which ran alongside the track from Withcall Tunnel. The water would be carried to the stations in all manner of containers, the favourite of which were milk churns.

Regular visitors using the line would include the stallion man, who made periodical visits to the farms along the line. The stallion man and his charge would travel in a specially designed stallion box with a compartment for the horse and an accommodation cabin attached in which the man would live and sleep during his tour of the area. The stallion boxes would be kept in goods sidings during the period the stallion was covering the local mares. The number of working horses in country areas was considerable and the railway company made great facilities available for this sort of trade. The arrival of the stallion man was a great event in the villages. Children would turn out to greet the stallion which would be decorated with ribbons, well groomed, with plaited tail, combed mane, polished harness and covered with horse brasses.

Another regular visitor would be the French onion man who would arrive at the villages with his onion-festooned bike. The onions would arrive by rail and be parked in a siding at Louth while the onion man worked the rounds of the local villages.

World War I saw the felling of many acres of pine trees around Withcall which were taken by rail and used for shoring up trenches on the battle fields of France and Belgium. After the almost total deforestation of Wales for this purpose, the Government began to turn to places like Withcall for trench props. Pit props were also supplied through Withcall, the more pulpy wood being supplied to the paper industry.

During World War II 233 Maintenance Unit had several railheads at stations along the line. These were used to supply armaments to the nearby aerodromes of "Bomber County". Wragby, South Willingham, Donington-on-Bain and Withcall were used for this purpose. Hallington was used as an empties dump. From here the assembled empty cases would be returned to the munitions factories.

233 Maintenance Unit had a bomb dump on the old Roman road between Caistor and Horncastle. Known as "Bomb Alley", the dump was guarded by soldiers with fixed bayonets stationed at every road junction. Thousands of tons of bombs destined for Hamburg and Cologne were stacked up on the grass verges as far as the eye could see. Civilians using this stretch of road had to produce a special pass before they could proceed. For several years the land was tilled and crops were harvested while farmers and their men could see stacks of 1,000 lb. bombs just over the hedges.

Most of the bombs delivered by rail came via Donington-on-Bain, which was perfectly suited for this kind of traffic due to the village's position in a valley and between two long tunnels. A quiet little wayside station, well-equipped with sidings, but from the air as difficult to find as a needle in a haystack, was the perfect spot for the RAF's bomb transit depot used to supply the many aerodromes of the Lincolnshire based bomber groups.

Bombs delivered to the transit depots along the line came in all shapes and sizes, from little four pounders to the giant 20,000 lb. "blockbusters". Mr Jones the station master at Donington at this time confirmed what a busy time the station had during the war. He said they often had two special bomb trains arrive at the station during a day and sometimes more. "After one big bomber raid," he said, "our stocks were nearly all exhausted. But there was a time when our yard and every other on the branch was filled up with bombs. We had thousands upon thousands of them."

On one occasion an important raid on Germany had to be cancelled because the engine delivering the required armaments was too large to get through Willingham Tunnel. The locomotive should have been changed for a smaller one at Lincoln.

Stan Fanthorpe recalled a near-disaster on the line in 1944. He was fireman to driver Priestly of Lincoln on an ex-GCR 'J11', "Pom-Pom". The train was in the charge of guard Sellars of Lincoln and consisted of 18 wagons destined for various stations along the Louth-Bardney branch. Every wagon contained one large bomb, the 18 wagons constituting a full load on the heavily graded line.

The first station at which wagons were detached was South Willingham. The engine went forward with five wagons, leaving the rest and the brakevan on the single line and coupled up to five empty wagons in the siding, with the intention of backing them onto the rest of the train. However, all that could be seen was the rest of the train disappearing down the incline in the direction of Bardney.

The runaway train ran through East Barkwith station and demolished the level crossing gates. Fortunately, communication was established with the signalman at Wragby who was able to open his crossing gates. He estimated the speed of the wagons at 40 mph as they passed through the station. The train finally came to rest in Kingthorpe Bottom, see-sawing itself to a standstill. The train crew and staff at Willingham feared that the runaway would collide with the Lincoln to Louth "pick-up" goods due on the branch at that time. Fortunately the train was still at Bardney.

Guard Sellars was held responsible for not securing the brakes on the train. Because of wartime restrictions on reporting the movements of armaments the incident was not reported in the press.

Not only had the line established itself as a centre of communications for the surrounding areas but its waste and unused bits and pieces of land were put to good use. As well as providing firewood old sleepers were used for building pig styes and the odd pocket of railway land used to build them on. Lineside land was cultivated, rhubarb, gooseberries and currants usually picked by the children to earn a bit of extra money. Brambles were picked and often sold to Ticklers factory for jam making.

On one part of the line an embankment was covered with white violets, reputedly the largest plot in Great Britain. Quite a trade built up between Withcall and the London flower markets. The London purchasers would send containers and white ribbon every year. Children would gather the flowers, tie them into bunches with the ribbon and pack them into the moss filled containers ready for the journey to London. As much as £5 could be made during the three week season. The violet money was often used by mothers to buy children's clothes.

Game in the form of rabbits, hares and partridge was trapped and killed along the line. Skins of rabbits and moles were sent to Abingdon in Oxfordshire and realised up to 2/6d. each. Traps and snares were used the length of the line, and there are many stories of railwaymen going to inspect their snares and finding themselves flat on their face caught in another snare. The gentle pace of life and infrequent trains along the line meant that locomotives could be stopped and snares inspected at leisure.

Bill Abbott, who was station master, signalman, porter and "general factotum" at Hallington during World War II further illustrates the general unhurried atmosphere of the line. The morning alarm on occasions would be the 7 am out of Louth whistling at Hallington distant signal giving Bill enough time to get out of bed, into his trousers, open the gates and catch the morning papers as they were thrown from the passing train. Bill also worked at Donington-on-Bain as signalman and estimated an average of 100 wagons a day being turned at the station during the War.

W. McGowan Gradon described a journey on the branch in 1946.

> Cutting through the southern end of the Lincolnshire Wolds, this picturesque branch, 21 miles in length, has several unusual features to commend it to the railway enthusiast. The scenery is delightful, and in complete contrast to the flatness usually associated with the greater part of the county.
>
> The branch leaves the main line just west of Bardney station, and curves away sharply to the north. Kingthorpe, the first station, 4 miles from Bardney, has a goods loop and a single platform. Wragby, the principal station on the line, and the only one boasting two platforms and a passing loop for passenger trains, is 2 miles beyond Kingthorpe. It has a fair sized goods yard which handles a considerable amount of agricultural traffic in normal times. So far, the line has passed through fairly level agricultural country, which continues for another 3 miles to East Barkwith where the southern edge of the Wolds can be seen from the down side of the line.
>
> After a short, sharp fall into East Barkwith station, which has a single platform and a goods loop, the line starts to climb towards the Wolds and gradients steepen to more than 1 in 70. Curving northeastwards, the track reaches South Willingham, 1¾ miles from East Barkwith. Here there is the usual single platform and short goods loop and short siding beyond the station. The line now turns almost due east, and, passing through a cutting in the folds of the hills, enters South Willingham tunnel, about ¾-mile long. Emerging from the tunnel the line drops sharply down a valley between the hills to Donington-on-Bain, 3 miles from South Willingham. Donington is a Staff station and there is a goods yard of similar size to that at Wragby. Although trains can be crossed here, the loop is not normally used and the station beyond has only one platform. Immediately beyond Donington the line starts to climb steeply, reaching a maximum gradient

'C12' No. 67379 awaits departure from Kingthorpe with the 3.57 pm from Louth; June 1951.   M. Black

A Bardney to Wragby "goods" passing the derelict Kingthorpe station in October 1959 hauled by 'J6' class No. 64219.   M. Black

Kingthorpe, looking towards Wragby, June 1951.   M. Black

Class 'C12' No. 67379 at Bardney with a Louth train, May 1951.   M. Black

The impressive nameboard at Bardney (June 1951).   M. Black

The Louth goods arriving at Bardney on 13th October, 1951, hauled by class 'J11' No. 64320. *P.H. Wells*

The branch platform and buildings at Bardney station, 1968. *Mowat Collection*

Bardney station looking west with a good view of the signal box.
Author's Collection

Bardney station looking west, showing the short branch line platform and with the island platform buildings demolished. *Author's Collection*

Bardney station viewed in October 1956. M. Black

An RCTS Railtour at Bardney, photographed from the signal box on 16th May, 1954. H.B. Priestley

Branch line stock at Bardney. Note the somersault signal. *N.E. Stead*

Class 'C12' No. 67379 on the 1.50 pm from Bardney to Louth, 3rd November, 1951. *M. Black*

A class of locomotive which may have been used on the Bardney line; GNR class 'F2' 0–4–2 No. 593. *Real Photographs (LGRP)*

Local traders wagon for Louth.
Courtesy Gloucester Carriage and Wagon Company

Sir Ronald Matthews after presenting medals to Constable Staley, Driver Ingoldmells, Goods Guard Dodman and Passed Cleaner Jackson.
LNER Magazine

The station staff at Wragby station and the crew of No. 67379 post for photographs on the last passenger train, 3rd November, 1951.   *Author's Collection*

of 1 in 65. The summit is reached about the middle of Withcall tunnel, 1 mile long, which carries the line through the last shoulder of the Wolds. Down to Withcall, 3 miles from Donington, the railway is carried on a series of embankments and round a number of sharp reverse curves, one of which has a long length of check rail. Withcall station stands on a gradient of 1 in 79 falling towards Louth. The layout is similar to that at South Willingham. From here the line gradually levels out into gently undulating farming country. Hallington, 1¾ miles from Withcall, is a replica of East Barkwith. Finally, the branch curves round to the north and joins the Boston–Grimsby main line less than ½-mile from Louth station, where there is a short bay platform on the up side to accommodate the branch trains. Except at Wragby, all the home and starting signals have the up and down arms mounted on the same post. Several of these have the lamps and spectacles placed much lower than the signal arms. At South Willingham all signals are left in the "off" position, except when there is any shunting taking place. Level crossings at the stations which are not block posts prevent this practice. A trip from Wragby to Louth and back on the footplate of 4–4–2 tank No. 4501 was an interesting experience. The train consisted of two close-coupled ex-Great Northern articulated coaches and an ex-North British eight-wheeler, built at Cowlairs in 1901. Although the train was of modest weight, the gradients made it quite a stiff task for the little 45 year-old engine. After the fire was made up at Bardney it was necessary to replenish it only three times: at Wragby, approaching Willingham tunnel, and at Donington-on-Bain. Steam pressure never fell below 155 lb. and on the down gradients some quite brisk running was done, with speeds of around 45 mph.

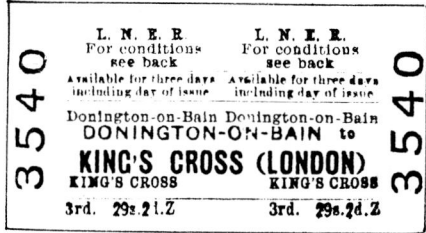

Chapter Four

The 1946 Explosion

Despite the line's close association with the war effort in Lincolnshire through the supply of armaments to the local air bases, it was not bombs which caused the 1946 explosion on the line.

The locomotive concerned was an old GN 'D3' No. 4317 based at Louth. The driver was Jack Ingoldmells, fireman Geoff Jackson and guard Arthur Dodman, all of Louth. The train was returning morning freight from Bardney to Louth and the locomotive was working hard out of South Willingham on the climb to High Street tunnel. A hot ember was thrown from the engine's chimney and landed in a wagon part-way along the train containing propane cylinders packed in straw. The straw ignited and was burning fiercely by the time the fire was noticed about a quarter of a mile outside Donington-on-Bain station. Geoff Jackson and Arthur Dodman isolated the burning wagon by detaching behind, drawing forward, uncoupling the blazing wagon and again drawing forward. The intense heat caused severe burns to both fireman and guard. By this time cylinder tops were being blown 200–300 yards. Arthur Dodman went to warn a nearby farmer of the risk of explosion. Before fireman Jackson could get clear the cylinders exploded, peppering his overalls with holes like those made by shot blast.

The explosion caused the vehicle to run back onto the rear portion of the train setting fire to several coal wagons.

The local fire brigade attended to the fire and an ambulance came from RAF Ludford to administer first aid. Geoff Jackson's burns caused him to be in bandages to hands, face and legs for six weeks of his three month leave from work.

The mid-day Louth to Bardney passenger train was terminated at Donington and returned to Louth with the injured crew.

For their bravery all three members of the crew were awarded the LNER Railway Medal in recognition of courage and resource. The medal was the railway equivalent of the George Cross or George Medal, and was presented to the three men at Kings Cross by LNER Chairman, Sir Ronald Matthews.

Apart from the 1946 explosion the line was trouble free. Landslips were not uncommon particularly in the area between South Willingham and Donington-on-Bain. The combination of a plentiful rabbit population digging into the soft sandy soil and heavy rain filling the burrows was usually the cause. Most were minor slips and did not interfere with the running of the railway. However, a bigger and potentially much more dangerous landslide occurred on the 21st July, 1939, close by the eastern end of High Street tunnel. The result of the landslide was seen by a traveller passing over a nearby road bridge. The track was covered for some distance and any train coming out of the tunnel would have certainly been derailed, with possible serious consequences in terms of lives. The passer-by acted quickly 'phoning Wragby station just in time to prevent a train already standing at the platform from leaving.

Chapter Five

The Final Days

The letter from British Railways announcing its plans to close the line to all traffic was read out to members of the Louth RDC at a meeting in March 1951. The Clerk, Mr L.A. Pitt read:

> For some years now the traffic passing over the branch line between Louth and Bardney has been diminishing and the position has been reached that there is such disparity between the cost of working the line that the Railway Executive has come to the conclusion that all train services, passenger and freight may have to be withdrawn. Alternative railway passenger and freight services are available at Louth and Bardney and the Road Haulage Executive have depots at Louth, Lincoln and Langworth. It is felt that these alternative services together with the existing bus services provided between Louth, Wragby, Bardney and Lincoln will be adequate to take the place of those proposed to withdraw.

The proposal to oppose the closure was put forward by Councillor C.H. Benton, who made the point that several things which did not pay were maintained for the public good. He made a particular reference to the delivery of coal; if it was no longer to be delivered by rail to the various stations, the cost to the consumer was bound to increase. Councillor Benton also pointed out the importance of the line to local farmers for the movement of sugar beet to the Bardney factory.

During the ensuing discussion the continued increasing cost of rail travel was offered as a reason for people not using the line regularly. The fact that buses did not run connecting services and that people living in Donington-on-Bain, for instance, relied upon the railway as a means of getting a connection for London trains were other points raised.

Finally the Councillors agreed with BR's proposal to close the line to passengers, but opposed its closure to freight traffic. They felt it absolutely essential that the line be maintained for the delivery of freight and the collection of produce from farms in that part of the Wolds. The objection to total closure was supported by 28 members and opposed by 6.

A week after the closure announcement by the Railway Executive many people would not believe that such a move could be contemplated. However, it was becoming more and more apparent that any objections which may have been put by residents in the area would be to little avail. "There is an urgent need to implement the decision of the Railway Executive" was the terse comment of the district commercial superintendent and a clear indication of BR's intentions.

Although the RDC had quoted the interest of local farmers as a reason for keeping the line open for freight, three influential members of the Farmers' Union residing in the area most affected by the closure, publicly declared that in the interest of economy they could not oppose the closure.

Due largely to BR's resolve to implement the Executive's decision and a weakening of local opposition, it was decided that the last passenger train on the line would be the 3.57pm on Saturday, November 3rd. Freight traffic, however, would continue to use the line for the time being, although it was now pretty obvious to all concerned that the writing was on the wall. The high cost of running even a small branch railway with the employment of signalmen, maintenance men as well as engine men, all of whom would have to be employed even if the service was cut to one train a day, was a stark fact apparent to even the most optimistic opponents of closure. People in this country had come to expect safety standards second to none, maintenance costs were high and had to be met by revenue; it was patently obvious from the beginning that the Bardney line was never in a position to do this. When its supply of passengers to the revenue earning main lines dried up, it, along with many other branches, began to live on borrowed time.

Local opinion, accepting the fate of the line, now began to press the authorities in the area for improved transport facilities between Louth and Lincoln covering as wide an area as possible for the villages.

Saturday, 3rd November saw the last passenger train run between Louth and Bardney. Appropriately the locomotive used was an old GNR 'C12' No. 67379. The driver was Bill "Bumper" Cartwright of Tennyson Road, Louth, the fireman, Fred Hardy, of St Bernards Avenue, Louth, and the guard, Cyril Thompson, of Linden Walk, Louth. Because the usual Louth–Bardney rolling stock was somewhat antiquated, it was, for the comfort of the passengers on this last journey, replaced by coaches borrowed from the Mablethorpe line, numbered E88090, E86048 and E82861. Another 'C12', No. 67352 was cleaned and standing by in Louth yard in case there was sufficient demand to fill more carriages. In this event 67352 would have double-headed with 67379. What a sight that would have been!

The journey began at 3.57pm from Louth, there were about 50 passengers aboard for the historic trip. Number 1 steam coal was used, usually reserved for long distance express trains.

At Bardney the enthusiasts were given the added bonus of being allowed to turn the locomotive on the turntable. The last ticket for the return journey to Louth was issued to relief station master H. Thacker. The *Lincolnshire Chronicle* reported the events at Wragby station:

> Heavy rain on Saturday evening did not dampen the enthusiasm of a small crowd of people who gathered on the dimly lit platform at Wragby station to see the last act in 75 years of history. It was just after 6.30 on Saturday that the last passenger train to use the Bardney to Louth line, pulled into Wragby station and the send off it was given – fireworks and cheering – were more in keeping with an opening rather than a closing.
>
> The front of the engine as it steamed slowly into the station indicated a passing however, for hanging on the smokebox door was a large wreath which bore the short inscription, "Born 1876 – Died 1951 In Memoriam."
>
> A number of railway enthusiasts made the last journey on Saturday, leaving Louth at 3.57pm and returning in the evening. The last two passengers to board the train at Wragby were Mrs Fanny Richardson and young Margaret Holmes, both of Willingham. The last ticket issued from the station was to East Barkwith and was purchased by an enthusiast. As a comparison the first ticket ever issued from Wragby was a first class to Leeds. Station master E.W. Savory said that in 1883 a first class ticket to Hull cost 7/7*d*. against 16/11*d*. today. Mr Savory will be leaving Wragby; at present he does not know his new station, but signalman C. Smeaton, who has been at Wragby for four years, has gone to Langworth. Also on duty for the last train was porter A. Bannister.

At Bardney the return to Louth began in heavy rain. At the various stops the passengers dismounted to see what was happening. At some of the stations fog detonators were placed on the line to say "goodbye to the old lady". All through the journey the strains of "Auld Lang Syne" were heard from the coach in which the Gainsborough Model Railway Society travelled.

A considerable crowd had gathered at Louth for the arrival of the 7.21 from Bardney. The 'C12' arrived dead on time. People crowded around the engine intent upon getting the autographs of the crew.

Among those taking part in the day's proceedings were Mr Walter Clark, for 40 years a signalman at Louth South box; Mr T. White, curator of the Louth Museum; Mr C. Webb, assistant district commercial superintendent; Mr W. Johnson, Louth station master; Mr

G.T. Emmerson, district locomotive inspector; and Mr L.A. Teather from Lincoln goods department.

The Lincolnshire area of the Railway Correspondence Society was represented by Mr W. Woolhouse, and Mr E. Thompson represented the London section of the Society. Also present were Mr E. Ingram, Louth fuel officer, and Mr D.G. Hinchcliffe, an official of the Gainsborough Model Railway Society, the Rev. I.F.S. Jones and Mr A.G. Bradley of Lincoln. Mr R.F. Youell, assistant lecturer in Physics at Leeds University, wrote to Louth Station regretting that his official duties prevented him from being present but enclosing a sum of money to pay for some of the last tickets to be issued. Seven year old Diana Hinchcliffe presented driver Cartwright and fireman Hardy with a bouquet of carnations.

The final passenger journey between Louth and Bardney meant a number of staff at Louth Shed (40C) would become redundant. These included three drivers, six firemen and six other grades including cleaners.

Chapter Six

Closure and Afterwards

After its closure to passengers the line continued as a freight only service until 1956, when, on the 17th September, the section between Louth and Donington was closed. The 1st December, 1958 saw the end of the section between Donington and Wragby and finally the Wragby to Bardney section closed on 1st February, 1960, 86 years after the Louth and Lincoln Railway opened the same section to freight in 1874.

Brian Gray recalls that as an eleven year old boy he discovered a disused permanent way trolley in Donington station yard. He and a group of friends spent a week of the Easter Holidays restoring the trolley. There were two possible rides on the line. One from close by High Street tunnel, the trolley just managing to roll into Donington station. The alternative and much more spectacular ride was a run from Withcall tunnel. The steep falling gradient to the west gave enough momentum to scale a short rising gradient before a death-defying 20 miles-an-hour descent through Donington station, across the River Bain, finally coming to a standstill near Benniworth House half a mile beyond the station. Rival and, no doubt, jealous gangs would on occasion alter points resulting in some alarming derailments.

Unfortunately, Brian Gray's trolley was the last vehicle to travel the Louth-Bardney rails before the track lifting machinery began moving out from Louth in January 1961.

Although the line officially closed in 1960 stories concerning the Bardney Branch Ghost Train came to our attention. The stories centred around Hallington station and described the sounds of an approaching train entering the station and blowing-off steam. Being devout sceptics we decided to investigate the story. On a fine summer evening in August 1969 we drove to Hallington station. The station house was inhabited by the local shepherd who kept his two sheep dogs in a kennel outside the old station yard. We found the shepherd and asked his permission to park our car in the yard. He steadfastly refused, saying he had to be up early in the morning and our presence would disturb the dogs, and possibly himself through their barking. On the subject of the ghost train he remained silent and refused to comment.

We parked our car further up the narrow lane facing the station. On our left was a field full of sheep. To our right a field of grass or meadow which appeared to be empty. It was a perfect summer evening, the air warm and still. We listened and waited silently. At about 11.45 the surrounding silence was broken by the faint sound of what seemed to be an approaching steam engine, very faint at first, and seemingly working hard as it climbed towards the station. The sound increased until it was possible to hear the occasional snatch of wagon couplings and the distinctive clank of rods. The sound seemed to come to us in waves, getting louder and louder then fading away as if carried by a swirling wind. I think we must have sat there mesmerised until the barking of the dogs brought us back to our senses. I noticed the sheep had stampeded to the far side of the field.

The sound continued now very faintly as if moving towards Withcall, the dogs stopped barking and the sheep began to settle again.

We must have been very fortunate indeed because, although the stories continued, several friends have visited the scene but nothing has occurred to give them any satisfaction. The local farmer had installed a grain dryer in the immediate area, which may have had some bearing upon the ghostly train's inability to be heard again. We felt very fortunate to have heard the "Phantom Goods", which frustrated us by being unseen, but rewarded us by the fact that we had clearly heard its efforts.

Chapter Seven
The Line Today

Despite the fact that over twenty-five years have elapsed since the track was lifted it is still relatively easy to follow the course of the line. The Louth end is a bit blurred; the station, although still there, is in a pitiful state of decay. Plans are in hand to renovate it although its future use is unclear. It is now in the middle of a development area which occupies the old station yard, sidings, site of the shed and trackbed.

Beyond Louth perhaps the easiest place to pick up the trackbed is a road bridge on the A153. The line passes under the bridge and heads west steadily climbing towards Hallington which is visible in the distance.

Most of the line is now owned by farmers who use much of it as farm roads. I have walked most of it, observing the usual courtesies, and have not yet found myself at the wrong end of a 12 bore!

Hallington station is an easy starting point heading west towards Withcall, the steady climb continues beyond Withcall to Withcall tunnel about a mile beyond the station.

Access to the most spectacular part of the line is by means of the former station yard at Donington-on-Bain. The yard is now owned by a farmer and a huge building has been erected at the western end of the yard. Heading west from Donington-on-Bain towards Willingham tunnel takes the traveller through some beautiful countryside, across an embankment and through a rich red sandstone cutting planted with pine trees and bracken. Recently the road overbridge immediately to the east of Donington-on-Bain station has been infilled.

Both tunnels are still in evidence and still complete although their fabric has obviously somewhat deteriorated.

With the single exception of Kingthorpe, of which all evidence has been wiped from the face of the earth, the station buildings remain and most are in good order and little changed from the original. Even Withcall's tiny wooden station building still stands, now used as a Methodist Chapel.

Bardney is now isolated from both Boston and Lincoln, the station building still stands with the short branch platform still in evidence; the site is now owned by the British Sugar Corporation.

One remarkable thing about this line is the quality and substantial nature of the station buildings. Although the line was single throughout its life, the stations are hardly what one would call country halts except Withcall. The rest are brick-built solid buildings which seem to suggest something more than a single line branch meandering through the Lincolnshire Wolds.

It has been suggested that the DMU could perhaps have saved the line. We doubt it; they ran on the Louth–Mablethorpe line and, although that was always a better financial proposition compared with the Louth–Bardney, it too closed in the 1960s.

The only salvation for the Louth to Bardney line, or at least part of it, would have been preservation for which the line would have been excellent, single track already, plenty of good station buildings and scenery second to none. Because much of the trackbed was laid on an ash base it is still in very good condition and mainly weed free; relaying would present few problems. Unfortunately the trackbed is now back firmly in the hands of the farmers who, even the minority making sympathetic noises, have no intention of returning any part of it to its former glory – which is a bit hard on the "old lady" who served their needs in particular for over 80 years.

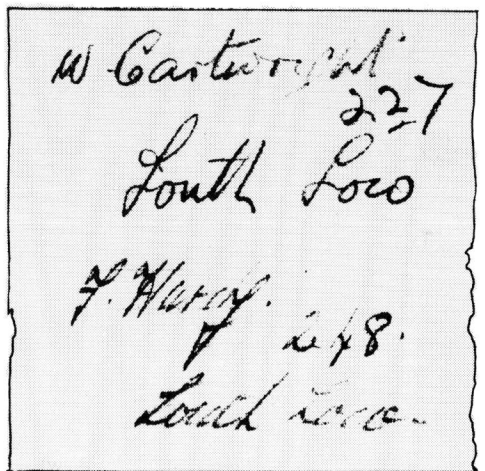

(18)
Great Northern Railway
TO
BARDNEY

Appendix One

Louth to Bardney Engineering Works

Bridge No.	Local name or description	Mileage ex Kings X	U – under O – over	Date of construction
	Culvert			1873
	Culvert			1873
	Culvert, Sewerage Dyke	129.58		1873
	Culvert			1873
1	Tilehouse Beck Bridge	130.54	U	1873 brick abutments and arch, span 17'2"
2	Tilehouse Road Bridge	130.60	O	1873 brick abutments and arch, span 16'6"
3	Kingthorpe Beck Bridge	133.13	U	1873 brick abutments and arch, span 13'10". Longitudes under each rail, 4" planking
	KINGTHORPE STATION			
4	Kingthorpe Road Bridge	133.17	O public	1873 brick abutments and arch, span 15' (15'5" on the skew)
5	Kingthorpe Beck Bridge	133.27	U	1873 brick abutments 13"x12" longitudes under each rail 4" planking
6	Wragby Beck Bridge	133.62	U	as above
7	Wragby Beck Bridge	134.06	U	as above except 3" planking
8	Wragby Beck Bridge	134.39	U	as above
	Culvert	135.03	U	
	WRAGBY STATION			
	Culvert	136.56	U	
	EAST BARKWITH STATION			
9	Cattle Creep Bridge	139.36	U occupation	1873 brick abutments 14"x14" longitudes under each rail 4" planking, 8'8" span
	SOUTH WILLINGHAM STATION			
	Culvert	139.74	U	1873 5' span (5'7" on the skew)
	Culvert			4'9" deep. Brick with invert 1'6" span, 2'6" deep
10	South Willingham Road Bridge	139.75	U public	1873 stone abutments and wing walls, brick arch, span 25' (27'6" on the skew)
	South Willingham Tunnel	140.57–141.30		1874 brickwork; span at rail level 14', maximum span 14'10", headway at centre 15'11". Length 558 yards.
11	Cawdal Lane Bridge	141.18	O public	1874 as for No.10, span 14'6" (15'6" on the skew)
12	Bain River Bridge	142.10	U	1873 as above, span 9'6" (11'4" on the skew)
	Culvert	142.35	U	
13	Cattle Creep Bridge	142.36	U occupation	1873 as above, span 12'
	DONINGTON-ON-BAIN STATION			

Louth to Bardney Engineering Works (continued)

Bridge No.	Local name or description	Mileage ex Kings X	U – under O – over	Date of construction
14	Donington High Road Bridge	142.70	O public	1873 as above, span 14'10"
15	Cattle Creep Bridge	143.53	U occupation	1873 as above, span 14'8"
	Culvert	143.53	U	1873 brick, egg shaped
16	Cattle Creep Bridge	144.01	U occupation	1873 as for 10, span 9'7"
	Withcall Tunnel	144.12–144.56		1873 brickwork; span at rail level 14'10", maximum span 15'3½", headway at centre 14'3½", length 971 yards
17	Cattle Creep Bridge	144.70	U occupation	1873 as for 10, span 11'6"
	Culvert	145.50	U	
18	Cattle Creep Bridge	145.50	U occupation	1874 brick abutments, stone wing walls & brick arch, span 13'2" (13'8" on the skew)
	WITHCALL STATION Culvert	146.72	U	
19	Cattle Creep Bridge	147.06	U occupation	1874 brick abutments, 13½"x13½" longitudes under each rail, 3" planking
	Culvert	147.16	U	1874 1'8" diameter
	HALLINGTON STATION Culvert	148.04	U	1874 span 6' (6'5" skew), 5'9" deep
20	Horncastle Road Bridge	148.32	O public	1874 brick abutments and arch, span 14'11" (23'10" on the skew)
	Culvert	148.69	U	1872
21	London Road Bridge	149.20	O public	1872 brick abutments and arch, span 14'10"
	Culvert			
	Culvert			
22	Alford Road Bridge	149.53	O public	1872 brick abutments and arch, span 14'11" (15'3½" on the skew)

Extracts from the GNR Engineer's book of reports on structures circa 1900.

Appendix Two

Signalling Plans of Intermediate Stations

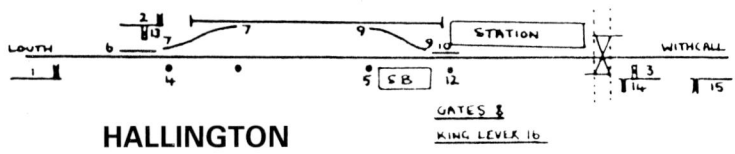

HALLINGTON

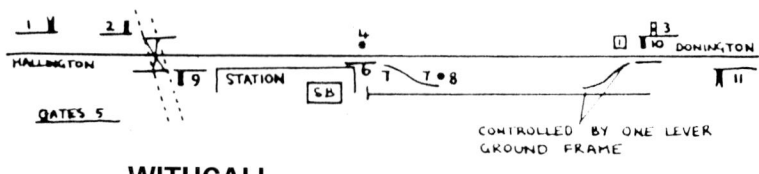

WITHCALL

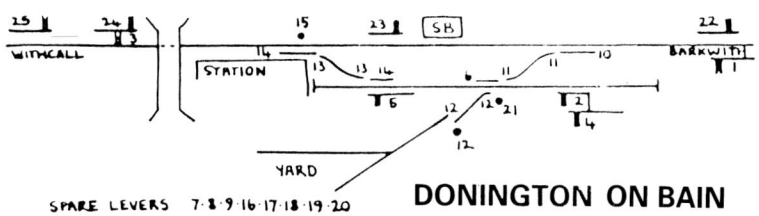

DONINGTON ON BAIN

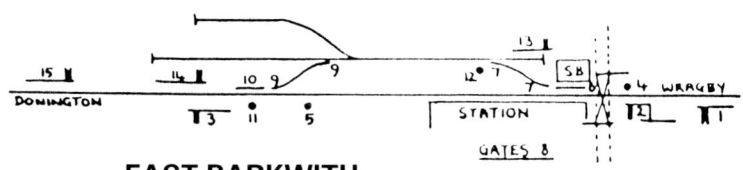

EAST BARKWITH

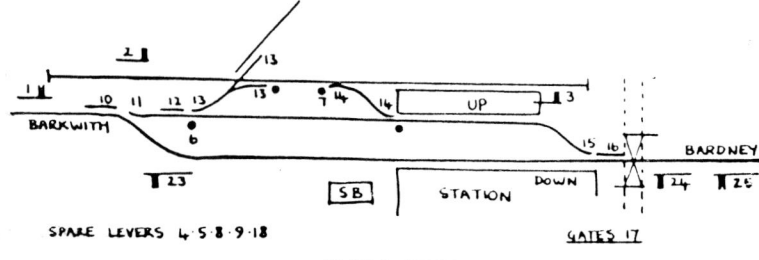

WRAGBY